# College Admissions and the Public Interest

# College Admissions and the Public Interest

B. Alden Thresher

College Entrance Examination Board, New York
1989

Reprinted, with new Introduction, 1989.

Inquiries regarding this book should be addressed to
Editorial Office, The College Board,
45 Columbus Avenue, New York, New York 10023-6992.

Additional copies of this book may be ordered from
College Board Publications, Box 886,
New York, New York 10101-0886. The price is $12.95.

ISBN: 087447-351-9

Library of Congress Catalog Card Number: 89-062663

Printed in the United States of America.

# Introduction

*In 1988, the College Board began a systematic reassessment of the theory and practice of college admissions in the United States. The republication in 1989 of* College Admissions and the Public Interest, *written by B. Alden Thresher and originally published by the Board in 1966, is the first step in what will be a long process of analysis, publication, and renewal. With the exception of the Introduction, the text of this new paperback edition remains unchanged from the original 1966 hardcover edition. Thresher's book is where the professional practice of admissions begins. The goal now is to understand this beginning, and to apply anew the fundamental principles that Thresher discovered and taught, and at the same time to prepare ourselves, our colleges and universities, and our students, for next steps in the direction of education in the public interest.*

*B. Alden Thresher was long regarded as an elder statesman of admissions, guidance, and testing. He was chairman of the College Entrance Examination Board from 1958 to 1960, and was also a member of the board of Educational Testing Service for four years thereafter.*

*He joined MIT in 1929 as instructor in economics, and in 1935 was appointed associate professor. In 1936 he became director of admissions at MIT, a post he held for 25 years until his retirement, when he was named professor emeritus. During his tenure as director of admissions he was also appointed professor of economics. Professor Thresher died in 1984.*

In August 1975, with no particular background or preparation for the assignment, I became an admissions officer. On my first day I met Jean Rayburn, a veteran admissions officer who eventually became a close friend and colleague, and we sat down together to discuss what I was to do. Jean asked how much I knew. I replied that I knew next to nothing. I had never made a school visit, read an applicant's folder, sat in an admissions committee meeting, or done anything else related to admissions. Indeed, I had wondered throughout the job interview what the president meant by "legacy," "predictive ability," "validity study," and a host of other terms I had not heard before. Jean listened for a while. Then she said, "What you need is some time with my friend Thresher."

Later that day, Jean brought me the book that you have before you, and her friend Thresher became my friend, as well.

*College Admissions and the Public Interest* is at one and the same time the best of guides to the practice of admissions (and counseling, and the administration of financial aid, and a dozen other functions that support education), and sustains the most compelling of arguments that education should be built on the student's interests rather than those of society, a faculty, or an institution. A deceptively simple and direct book, it argues in plain English for a view of education that is both pragmatic and idealistic.

The book was a success in its time. It touched a nerve by its suggestions of why so many talented students did not choose college; by its understanding of what higher education might hope to accomplish in our time; and by its insistence that institutions and their people failed because they forgot what really matters, not because their students failed them. Moreover, just as admissions reached maturity as a profession in the colleges and universities, Thresher's book told admissions officers what their profession ought to accomplish.

The book still matters. Its essential assertion that education must serve the student first and the institution, its faculty, or society second, forces us to examine how and why we do what we do. Its commonsensical, modest approach to counseling and advising sets a standard for anyone who wants above all to enable students to accomplish whatever they can and will. In 1966, this approach shaped the admissions profession. Today, it can keep us honest.

Thresher drew ideas and inspirations for his book from a dozen sources —from Alfred North Whitehead, from economic theorists, from contemporary scholars of American education, from educational systems in other countries, and even from a philosopher of science. From each source was derived a special contribution toward a unitary understanding of what admissions ought to accomplish, and why.

Thresher believed that the business of education was to serve students, and that institutions and people who work in them rarely act out of concern for the interests of students. He believed that it was the mission of counselors and admissions officers to understand the whole system of education, and to use that understanding to assist the students who use those services. Anything less, he argued, betrayed the public interest.

Part of the pleasure of having known Thresher was his gentle command of the language. Never verbose or preachy, and only rarely pedantic (and then in none but the best of causes), Thresher was the soul of good sense and dispassion. Mocking arrogance in educational leaders, he urged the admissions officer to take with a grain of salt "supply side" theories of education. In beginning his argument against exclusivity as a value in education, Thresher warned that our universities were often "unregenerate, unreconstructed, and complacent," places where "such harmless foibles as medieval regalia are too often accompanied by medieval habits of thought."

Another part of the pleasure of having known Thresher was that his blunt phrases often led to profound understandings of education itself. "College," he said, "is to be a crutch, not a stretcher." "Snobbery is endemic in the human species," and "[education]...has always been a favorite vehicle of snobbishness."

Yet Thresher's aim was never to be clever. Rather, he argued for education grounded in students' needs and capacities, for admissions decisions made by people who understood their own motives and acted above them, and for education that taught students how to teach themselves. At the same time, he argued against much that we may have taken for granted, against institutional and individual arrogance, against selectivity based on the notion that exclusivity at the point of admission proved the worth of an education, and against classbound or racist ideas of those who ought to go to college (and which college), and those who ought not.

In each of these biases, Thresher saw clearly what lay before him. In 1966 he identified the failings of universities and colleges during the years when student unrest grew. He demonstrated the analogy between exclusion of black students from American institutions of higher education and exclusion of working-class students from European universities. He foresaw the rise of community colleges and other open-enrollment colleges to meet fundamental and demographic needs, and he tied the rise of open-enrollment colleges to self-delusion and, indeed, failure in the more traditional colleges and universities.

In the end, the book's value may be a simple truth. Thresher argued for what he himself was: a knowledgeable person of good will and sound capacity to reason, devoted to students and to education, who acted from the conviction that the public interest required the best of him. A person with these qualities, in Thresher's view, really ought to be an admissions officer.

Students need men and women like Thresher now, and what students need is the surest definition of the public interest.

Thresher's book remains after some 23 years the single, most useful guide to the practice of admissions, and the most compelling argument for fundamental reforms of much of our practice within higher education. It defines the issues of today as well as it did the issues of the late 1960s, different though the two eras may be. It demonstrates what we ought to be.

*John T. Casteen, III*
President,
The University of Connecticut

# College Admissions and the Public Interest

B. Alden Thresher
*Director of Admissions Emeritus, Massachusetts Institute of Technology*

College Entrance Examination Board, New York
1966

# Foreword

Coming from academic beginnings in economics, the dismal science, the author of this essay presided for 25 years over the admissions program of a famous institute of technology. As everyone knows, it is the business and special pleasure of admissions officers to thwart the legitimate aspirations of the young. Their professional tools are the computer, multiple-choice tests, and a cultivated disregard for the complexities of humanity. Under these circumstances, this book should have been a statistical treatise or at least a manual on efficient office procedures. It is nothing of the kind—the title is precise.

The fact is that over a distinguished career Professor Thresher accumulated all the credentials necessary to qualify him as the dean of his profession. A further fact is that he has invariably seen his job in the broadest and only useful perspective—that of social process and the public interest.

It is particularly appropriate that the College Entrance Examination Board should publish this book. Mr. Thresher has been chairman of the College Board and has been one of perhaps half a dozen men who have shaped the Board's present structure. But even if the author and the Board had never met, the book would have to be published, for it discusses the things that are important in college admissions but are frequently ignored or misunderstood.

In his career, the author has shown that the conduct of admissions is a fit undertaking for reasonable men. In this book he tells why.

*S. A. Kendrick*
Executive Associate
College Entrance Examination Board

# Contents

Preface . . . . . . . . . . . . . . . . . . . . . . . . . . . . . . . . . . . . . . . . . 1

1. Admissions as a Social Process . . . . . . . . . . . . . . . . . 3
A "Great Sorting" . . . . . . . . . . . . . . . . . . . . . . . . . . . . . . . . 3
The Supply of Talent . . . . . . . . . . . . . . . . . . . . . . . . . . . . . 9
The Demand for Talent . . . . . . . . . . . . . . . . . . . . . . . . . . . 15
Scarcity and Selection . . . . . . . . . . . . . . . . . . . . . . . . . . . . 18
Levels of Analysis . . . . . . . . . . . . . . . . . . . . . . . . . . . . . . . 25

2. The Student and His Future . . . . . . . . . . . . . . . . . . . 28
Focus of Decision . . . . . . . . . . . . . . . . . . . . . . . . . . . . . . . 28
The Inarticulate Major Premise . . . . . . . . . . . . . . . . . . . . . 29
The Cultural Matrix . . . . . . . . . . . . . . . . . . . . . . . . . . . . . . 30
The Useful and the Poetic . . . . . . . . . . . . . . . . . . . . . . . . . 33
Kinds of Intervention . . . . . . . . . . . . . . . . . . . . . . . . . . . . 36
Education as a Cultural Complex . . . . . . . . . . . . . . . . . . . . 41
Constriction at the Roots . . . . . . . . . . . . . . . . . . . . . . . . . . 43

3. Admissions within the Walls . . . . . . . . . . . . . . . . . . . 47
Faculty Viewpoint . . . . . . . . . . . . . . . . . . . . . . . . . . . . . . . 47
Admissions Officers Emerge . . . . . . . . . . . . . . . . . . . . . . . 51
Registrar and Admissions . . . . . . . . . . . . . . . . . . . . . . . . . 54
Selection Problems . . . . . . . . . . . . . . . . . . . . . . . . . . . . . . 55
Organization of Admissions . . . . . . . . . . . . . . . . . . . . . . . 59

4. College Admissions as a System . . . . . . . . . . . . . . . . 66
The System Concept . . . . . . . . . . . . . . . . . . . . . . . . . . . . . 66
Abandoned Clienteles . . . . . . . . . . . . . . . . . . . . . . . . . . . . 71
Ignorant Selection . . . . . . . . . . . . . . . . . . . . . . . . . . . . . . . 74
Value—and "Value Added" . . . . . . . . . . . . . . . . . . . . . . . . 75
Models of Student Distribution . . . . . . . . . . . . . . . . . . . . . 76
Optimum Distribution . . . . . . . . . . . . . . . . . . . . . . . . . . . . 83

Notes . . . . . . . . . . . . . . . . . . . . . . . . . . . . . . . . . . . . . . . . 88

# Preface

This essay deals with some of the broader aspects of the college admissions process in the United States. It will not tell the reader how to get into college or how to run a college admissions office. Having spent some years in charge of a selective admissions operation, the author is keenly aware of the pitfalls that lie in wait for anyone who presumes to select from among large numbers of promising youngsters those who will prove best qualified for any given life work, or even to identify those who will finish a four-year undergraduate course.

The central thesis of these pages is threefold: first, one cannot tell by looking at a toad how far he will jump; second, the process of admission to college is more sociologically than intellectually determined; and third, to understand the process one must look beyond the purview of the individual college and consider the interaction of all institutions with the society that generates and sustains them.

Perhaps these comments may aid admissions and guidance people by directing their attention beyond the normal boundaries of their daily concerns, or help concerned citizens who, having been through the college admissions process with their children, may wish to look more broadly at the educational enterprise in the light of the public interest.

*B. Alden Thresher*
Cambridge, Massachusetts

# 1. Admissions as a Social Process

## A "Great Sorting"

Of the two million boys and girls who graduate from high schools each year in the United States, more than half distribute themselves among some 2,000 colleges, universities, junior colleges, and technical institutes. This "great sorting" is a social process of great complexity, not fully understood by the students themselves, by their parents and advisers, or by the educators, including admissions officers, who participate in it. The sorting process, taken in its entirety, is a product of an immense number of individual choices and decisions taken by millions of people, under the influence in part of calculations and estimates projected a generation into the future and in part of beliefs, opinions, whims, ancient loyalties, and areas of ignorance scarcely amenable to rational estimate. It is important to note that most of the decisions involved occur outside college admissions offices, not in them. Access to higher education is essentially a social process deeply involved with the society's entire cultural pattern and system of values.

Each student is considering whether to go to college, or seeking a college that might meet his needs, evaluating and appraising it as best he can, and narrowing down to a choice. Colleges, conversely, are on the lookout for recruits, exercising a choice among them, sometimes stringently, sometimes very mildly indeed. In the market for higher education, just as in the job market or the marriage market, the processes of search, appraisal, and selection go on continuously, on both sides, and emphases shift according to reciprocal needs and scarcities. In the past it has been broadly true that it was students who selected colleges; they still do, but it is becoming apparent that now, to an increasing degree, colleges are also selecting students.

The entire process of admission to college is conditioned by historical circumstances that have caused a sharp breaking point to occur at the end of the secondary school years. We now see this break, in one sense, as artificial and arbitrary. Education in the current perspective is coming to be thought of as a seamless web, a continuous cradle-to-grave affair. Even the span of formal education—roughly from nursery school through graduate or professional school—is but a part of the whole. We have learned to appreciate both the determinative importance of preschool experience for infants, and the continuity of growth and development made possible by adult education. So the location of the school-to-college breaking point, with the major reshuffling among students and institutions that occurs at this stage, is essentially arbitrary.

So intricate are the arrangements needed to make workable the business of getting into college that the practical tactics of admission often divert attention from the educational processes which are the heart of the whole matter. As in all complex and poorly understood social situations, unfounded beliefs, folklore, and old wives' tales grow spontaneously. Popular opinion about college admissions represents it as a screening based on intellectual achievement and promise. So it is, in part; but this is by no means the whole story. The sorting process involves the interaction of sociological forces of many kinds. Some are so familiar and so subtle in their operation as easily to escape notice; they come to be taken quite for granted, on the principle that the last thing a fish would ever notice is water. We probably exaggerate the part played by rational, intellectual standards because these other forces are partly hidden by the protective coloring of habit, use, and wont.

In admission to higher education there is a dual process of affiliation. On the one hand, the transactions involved constitute a kind of symbiosis that unites the world of higher education to the larger society that contains and interacts with it. On the other hand, the same transactions serve to connect the partially isolated society of a single nation with the cosmopolitan structure of the world of learning. These are social processes of the utmost complexity. The ways in which they work themselves out differ from nation to nation, but the basic social forces remain much the same everywhere.

One can, to be sure, regard admissions as coterminous with a minor range of administrative procedures, supported by formal and not very significant curricular delimitations. This viewpoint, all too prevalent in the past, misses the point. The view appropriate to contemporary thought is quite the contrary—that admissions must be looked at in the broadest possible context. The roots of higher education lie deep within the needs and aspirations of entire populations. The range of forces that determine the demand for education, regulate access to it, and define the values that maintain it, reflects some of the deepest values of the surrounding culture. In the "systems" view, admissions and its related phenomena are regarded in the light of these wider considerations.

We have gained a new insight, in the last 15 years, into the key importance of the conditions that control access to higher education. These conditions both determine and express the relationship between the educational system and the society that has generated it and contains and interacts with it.

As secondary education improves, and as gross disparities in articulation between its subject matter and that of higher education become fewer, such academic devices as "entrance requirements" play a diminishing role. Though the prim college regulations about preparation and prerequisites that have been evolving for three centuries were always intended as screening devices, most of the real screening has all along been done by the accidents of socioeconomic origins, early environment, and the various levels of aspiration habitually characterizing particular groups and subcultures. Reflecting the pluralistic nature of our society, these forces have today become more complicated but no less powerful. As entrance requirements in the older sense have diminished in importance, efforts have increased to select students on broad grounds of intellectual promise and aptitude, to understand the dynamics of personality as it affects motives and energy, and to trace the dimensions of human excellence beyond such deceptively simple, unidimensional quantities as school marks and test scores.

But there is much more to the problem than this; study of the individual student in isolation gives only partial answers. The deeper social forces uniting him to society remain dominant. The determining factors that control entry into higher education are rooted in the home and school environment of children from infancy on. What used to pass for "recruiting" on the part of colleges and universities is seen in our present perspective as a superficial effort to rearrange the educational destinations of the limited fraction of the population that had managed to reach the twelfth grade without having its potential for further education damaged or destroyed. Formal entrance requirements, through their long evolution, have resulted for the most part from rearrangements of material conventionally taught in secondary schools in each epoch. In form they were set by the colleges, but in fact they could not stray far from what the schools were currently doing.

The question of who attains higher education, then, is more than a matter of admissions requirements, or even of finances. It is a question of who does or should aspire to education. This aspiration, in turn, is more than just a function of degrees of talent. It depends deeply on the society's total concept of what education means and what it can be expected to accomplish. The "level of aspiration" of the adolescent depends in subtle ways upon his parental and neighborhood environment. These determine his ability to sense a connection between such spontaneous interests as his environment and education have aroused in him, and his expectations of a place in the world as he is able to conceive it. From this interplay his educational goals, if any, are generated. The climate of opinion in which he grows up is probably the most important determinant of his future, educational or otherwise. It is related to intellectual values but is determined even more powerfully by deeper and less rational influences at work in the society that nurtures him.

Social class, which we in the United States like to ignore, or take note of only shamefacedly, plays a powerful part in access to education. It is a paradox that in our society, relatively less stratified than that of Europe, the phenomenon of social class has been given more objective scientific study than there. In older societies, class and caste concepts can easily come to be taken so for granted as to seem a part of the order of nature. The western heritage of ideas about education is rooted in a class structure out of the feudal era, only partly modified by the mercantile age, the Industrial Revolution, and the growth of urban communities. Traditional views about higher education, in their European versions, as well as in countries influenced by European colonization, assume a social structure and a set of social views and expectations inappropriate to more fluid societies, including those of the developing countries.

Our generation has backed rather awkwardly into a recognition of the scope and significance of the "access-to-education" concept. American colleges and universities entered the twentieth century inheriting a quite restricted concept of the forces that did or should regulate admission to college. It was not until the development of the land-grant colleges and the state college and university systems that the true genius of the American version of higher education began to manifest itself.

The older eastern universities and independent colleges of liberal arts moved very deliberately. They initiated in the 1890s a process of standardizing the subjects of secondary education deemed essential as prerequisites for admission. The process involved was a dual one: on the one hand it was a relatively minor rearrangement of the conventionally accepted secondary school subjects—for example, agreement on what works of what classical authors should be read. On the other hand it embodied the persistent liberalizing tendency that brought in mathematics, modern languages, English, and science. Much of this tendency was traceable to the rise of the academies from 1800 on, and later to Eliot's broadening of electives at Harvard.

Despite the importance of these trends, they left largely untouched the underlying social issues. Accepted as a part of the natural order of things was the "pool of ability" concept, the belief that higher education was the prerogative of a small fraction of the annual crop of youngsters—a fraction drawn mainly from the well-to-do mercantile, industrial, and professional class. It had little impact on the populace at large, most of whom were assumed to be incapable of higher learning. The nineteenth-century heritage of a classical curriculum of limited relevance to contemporary life tightened this limitation. The refreshing stream of classical learning that had burst upon Europe with the Renaissance had shrunk in the nineteenth century to an attenuated and formalized remnant, a pinched and pedantic version of classical culture. The main impact of science was yet to come. In the society that was taking form after the Civil War, the central demand was for vigorous, practical men of action. Even the engineering schools, which were then beginning to develop, got along with a minimum of science, as befitted an economy whose rate of change and innovation was slow despite its vigorous expansion.

The secondary schools served much the same limited clientele as the colleges. It is true that the rise of the academies had brought a needed influx of more practical subject matter and an atmosphere of relevance to contemporary life. It is true also that the initial development of public high schools toward the close of the century envisioned them as "people's colleges." Despite these liberalizing influences, it remained true well into the twentieth century that for the most part only those seeking to enter college completed secondary education, and the curriculum was predominantly "college preparatory" in a quite traditional sense. The normal expectations of most ambitious and vigorous young men, ready to play their part in the life of their time, simply did not include college. College was for ministers, lawyers, and a few scholars, atypical and either underwritten or able to afford the luxury of study.

The land-grant colleges and the state universities were the unique and characteristic contribution of America to the stream of higher education in the western world. These, from the start, represented a philosophy, social and educational, at wide variance with the colonial college tradition. Theirs was much more nearly an "open-door" policy, tempered by common sense provisions to exclude those clearly unsuited or unready for higher education. That universities of great distinction and the highest intellectual standards have sprung from this tradition is by itself enough to give pause to those who would push selectivity in admissions to ever greater extremes.

# The Supply of Talent

The simplest schematization of "the great sorting" would treat it as a matter of the supply of and demand for students—a convenient though greatly oversimplified concept.

On the one hand is the American society sending forward its annual crop of young people. Facing these young people stands a system of higher education more varied in its origins, more diversified in its auspices and management, more chaotic in its atomized separation, covering a wider range of "standards," and possessing, perhaps, more vitality than any in the world. This is the "supply" side of the educational process.[1] The ways in which these youth are drawn back after varying lengths of time into the social complex of the economy constitute the "demand" side. Considerations from the demand side, such as employability, economic productivity, manpower distribution, and social mobility constantly reflect back to the supply side of the equation. The interaction of these social complexes generates powerful forces. The admissions process acts as a kind of hinge point through which many of these stresses are transmitted. So the procedures connected with admissions, viewed in their full significance, are much more than a series of rules and customs. Through them are conducted social stresses, the study of which can tell much about the processes of the society that contains them.

The educational establishment, embedded in the social process, interacts with it not only by the inflow and outflow of students. It reflects the values and preoccupations of the society and cannot easily rise above them. Yet it is the critic of these values and preoccupations. In its rare and fortunate periods education, despite its innate tendency to conservatism, may play the part of stimulant and innovator. The institutionalized and routinized aspects of education, as of any basic function in society, are indispensable to practical continuity and effectiveness. Yet it is the critical and innovative aspects that generate growth and renewal, vision and change, in the happy epochs when these forces can break through the encrustations of tradition, organizational rigidities, and the vested interests of those who are comfortably lodged in ledges and crevices of the existing structure.

In recent years there has been a radical shift in viewpoint with regard to the broad social problem of access to higher education—that is, the supply side of the equation. This shift in turn has led to a changed view of the admissions function. Inspection of admissions credentials had been thought of traditionally as belonging to the more routinized aspect of education, and it therefore seemed natural in many colleges to put admissions under the direction of the registrar, to be looked after as a detail of academic accounting. Only in recent years have the social as well as the educational complexities involved in access to higher education come to be realized in anything like their full significance. The academic records aspect, though by no means negligible, has been dwarfed by comparison.[2]

Faint adumbrations of this newer attitude began as early as the 1920s when a few universities appointed officers who were to be specifically concerned with undergraduate admissions problems. The practice spread during the depression years of the 1930s, influenced more by the practical necessity to recruit freshmen in an era when cash customers were scarce than by any broader understanding of the social roots of education. Admissions committees continued the administration of academic requirements, but this sedate activity was quite overshadowed, particularly in the smaller, struggling colleges, by the strenuous sales effort necessary to recruit a freshman class. Field representatives of various kinds, some paid on commission, enabled colleges close to the margin of financial survival to track down and sign up new freshmen.

The wave of postwar enrollments from 1945 to 1950 temporarily reduced the need for active recruiting. After this wave subsided, the small colleges again had to struggle to fill their classes, though the more sought-after colleges, including those in the large, endowed universities, were able to exercise an increasing degree of selectivity. Many state-supported institutions, access to which had been easy, began to tighten their requirements. Tests for admission came to be more widely used in what had been virtually "open-door" colleges.

After 1950 a new set of ideas began to take hold. The question "Who should go to college?" began to be asked, and the possible answers seriously investigated. In the early stages this question carried overtones of discontent, on the part of the academic world, with the motivation and attitudes of many college students. Stress was put on the number of students in college who, it was thought, might better be elsewhere. Swayed by the contemporary playboy ethos, even students capable of solid achievement sometimes wasted their time and that of the faculty. College faculties making these complaints seldom paused to consider whether some part of the disaffection might be traceable to a curriculum that seemed to the student remote from his concerns, to pedantic and dull teaching, or to an authoritarian atmosphere that discouraged both innovation and inquiry.

Very soon the emphasis changed. Studies like that of Byron S. Hollinshead[3] began to show that a large proportion of youth of high ability simply were not continuing into higher education. The waste involved far exceeded that of carrying along into college some idlers who did not exert themselves. From our present perspective the waste of talent is even more serious than had been thought, because these studies looked primarily at "talent" identified as such and visible at or near the end of the high school course. Because talent pinched off at earlier stages simply remained invisible to scrutiny directed at the twelfth-grade level, it became easy to assume that only a small minority were capable of higher education.

A little later, studies like those of Ralph F. Berdie[4] cast doubt upon another easy assumption: that the main obstacle to further education was financial. The standard remedy had been to offer scholarships. If takers did not immediately appear, it was simple to conclude that those who were unresponsive were not seriously interested in further education, and so, clearly, not of "college caliber." Berdie and those who followed him established the basic fact that only about half of this "lost" talent was deterred solely by lack of money. The other half, in the phrase of that era, lacked "motivation," a convenient word that explains nothing. What these studies disclosed was the range of social forces that caused many youngsters of high ability to shun higher education. These would still not have gone to college even if they had had the money. Nothing in their experience had persuaded them that college would be a good idea, or indeed would have any relevance to their life or needs.

In the 1950s the term "talent search" came to represent a slightly more advanced stage in public understanding about education.[5] It marked the passing of the primitive notion that if one simply rang the bell and offered money for scholarships to all comers, any student worth helping would automatically appear, and that those who did not grasp at this opportunity were simply not worth wasting time on. It marked the first widespread departure from the notion that the only youngsters able to cope with higher education are those who know enough about it to want it. Talent, it began to appear, had to be searched out, helped, and encouraged. In large measure, it had to be created, granted some minimum initial endowment of native intelligence.

So the concept of the "search for talent," useful as a step in the evolution of thought, has yielded to repeated demonstrations that talent must be nurtured and encouraged at every stage if it is to survive and blossom—that talent, in fact, comes closer to being something produced than something stumbled upon and uncovered. This concept is broadly true, though here and there a nugget of pure genius turns up against all the odds. Access to education in Europe has always been organized traditionally along lines that implied a "pool of ability" manpower theory. It is significant that the Robbins Report in England explicitly disavowed this doctrine in 1963 and recognized the wide elasticity of the supply of able students, given the necessary conditions.[6] To be sure, not all children are equally bright. There is a genetic factor of great importance. But we simply do not know how to separate the genetic from the environmental component. We do know that intelligence, within far wider limits than anyone had suspected, can be increased by a favorable early environment, or stunted by a bad one. This is a conclusion of the first importance for a society like ours, already pressing hard against the limits of its educated manpower and desperately in need of more. Major social factors such as these we may call "conditions of opportunity." They are the most important determinants of who goes to college and where. A "condition" may be either a help or a constraint, a barrier or a highway.

For the first time, the overwhelming importance of an adolescent's self-image and level of aspiration began to be grasped. What had been obvious all along, but seldom appreciated or acted upon, began to penetrate public consciousness: that a major part of the preparation and predisposition for higher education occurs at home and during childhood, and that fairly specific habits, values, and attitudes are required. If these are lacking, few will surmount the handicap. The majority will be permanently blighted from realizing their potentialities or contributing as they might to society. All this began to undermine the assumption that "the really able will overcome all obstacles." The assumption had been based on no evidence except the observation that there were, indeed, a few who did overcome all obstacles. The evidence had become convincing that this lazy assumption had been wrong, and that a serious waste of human potential had resulted.

A major turning point was the Demonstration Guidance Project in Junior High School 43 and George Washington High School, both in New York.[7] It showed, in brief, that starting even as late as the seventh grade, a combination of enriched teaching, dedicated counseling and encouragement, and a determined effort to interest and involve parents, could produce remarkable results (at a moderate increase in per pupil expenditure), even in children from culturally deprived and poverty-stricken environments. Most of all, it showed that the operative force in this process was the change in the student's image of himself—a rise in his level of aspiration. This rise is the psychic power house; it provides the emotional energy and involvement without which the illumination of learning has little effect. These were boys and girls who had, as a matter of course, assumed that they would be carrying on a marginal, struggling existence; most of their windows on the world would be closed and shuttered, and they would be only dimly aware of the closing. They would join the great army of the alienated, strangers, never at home in society.

Through this program some benefited only a little; the average showed a marked improvement, and a substantial number came to see themselves as having powers and potential. They began to see that doors they never dreamed existed could be opened. A dramatic drop in juvenile delinquency occurred in these so-called slum schools.

These teen-agers underwent a true revolution of identity—the acquisition of a self-concept that gave them status, hope, and a respected place in a scheme of things they could begin to understand. Little enough is known, still, about the nature of these powerful psychosocial forces. But it is clearly in this area that we must look for the energies needed to bring about broad and fruitful access to higher education. The machinery of selection, recruiting, tests, classification, and the like remains useful and significant. But the true "nuclear" forces of the personality, which have begun to be tapped in these efforts with deprived children, lie at the root of the really basic problems of admission to college. By contrast, the worries of the prosperous middle-class youngster about getting into the "college of his choice" are of minor significance.

A generation ago, college admissions conventionally dealt with that small fraction of the twelfth-grade age group that was "college bound" and visible as such. That this should be a tiny minority was too often thoughtlessly accepted as a fact of nature. In current perspective this fact is seen, rather, to be due to serious defects in the educational system and in social attitudes. There will always be different levels of ability; not all students will be capable of high intellectual effort. But society thus far has scarcely made a serious effort to develop the talent it already demonstrably possesses. Nor has there been more than a little progress in fathoming the dimensions of human ability other than intellectual.

A certain broadening in the concepts that govern the admissions process has indeed occurred. Efforts have been made to assess "nonintellectual" qualities, to study biographical data, to experiment with "personality" tests, and to understand creativity. But the focus in all these efforts has been upon the individual. The atomized concept of the candidate as he stands, "on the hoof," has been the dominant one. Little attention, by contrast, has been paid to the social forces that sway groups of individuals and entire subcultures. We have been picking and choosing among the passive victims of vast, complex, and largely blind social processes. There has been only a little progress in understanding these processes, and less still in controlling them.

A society that has learned to raise the kinds of turkeys, cattle, or swine that it needs is largely released from the need for gathering roots and berries upon which to subsist. Yet for its most basic asset, underlying all others, namely human ability, it relies very largely on the kind of chancy "search-and-pick-up" technique appropriate to a tribe of digger Indians. It is true that "eugenics," in Francis Galton's sense of selective human breeding, has long been discredited; in fact it is unnecessary. The pool of genes from which society replenishes itself is almost infinitely varied and is perpetually renewed. "Nature is never spent." What we need is to make at least a beginning to develop adequately the talent we already have, which now falls so far short of its potential.

## The Demand for Talent

What forces resulting from society's demand for talent impinge on the problem of access to higher education? Overwhelmingly of first importance is the changing nature of the manpower problem and the demand of the employment market. At the turn of the century the small fraction of the age group who continued into higher education was made up primarily of those aiming at the traditional learned professions; to these were added a gradually growing fraction made up of scions of a prosperous business class affluent enough to devote some surplus to introducing its sons (and much more gradually its daughters) to polite letters, and to the deeper currents of learning then stirring under the influence of European university models. The rootlets were there, though still tiny: in science, from the time of Silliman at Yale; in graduate study on continental models, from the founding of Johns Hopkins; and in a group of schools like Rensselaer and M.I.T. that began to feed the rapid growth of industry and transport following the Civil War.

But all these beginnings were on a small scale. The vast economic growth of the country from the Civil War to World War I was managed with only a very small minority of college graduates. Prevailing opinion was content with this situation. Partly as cause, partly as a result, the college curriculum only slowly evolved out of the limited and pedantic version of classical studies which had come to characterize nineteenth-century America. The most powerful impulse for change from the demand side was the deep popular feeling for the pragmatic in education, which led first to the academies and later to the passage of the Morrill Act in 1862. The land-grant colleges and the state institutions modeled after them were, like the academies a century earlier, an expression of the deep need for relevance in education—relevance to the problems of a vigorous economy, an expanding frontier, a tide of immigration, an industrial revolution.

All this development is now history. The transformation of the job market, almost overnight, could scarcely have been foreseen a few years earlier. It seems hard to believe that as late as 1951 fears could be expressed that there would be a glut of college graduates—an over-educated group of unemployables, a white-collar proletariat.[8] World War II provided a turning point. It became obvious for the first time that the kinds of people turned out by the universities (and by the stronger undergraduate colleges) were overwhelmingly needed. In the era of the new developing countries, the Peace Corps, foreign aid, and the sophisticated technical needs of the age of space and automation, the university, on a worldwide basis, is seen above all as a producer of needed people. Often, indeed, they are so desperately needed as to distract attention from the very real weaknesses and defects in the conduct of higher education.

There is a kind of continued tension between the two major forces that keep the wheels of education turning. On the one hand a large majority of college students would admit quite frankly that the hope of a better job and a chance to rise in the world are their chief motives in seeking higher education. Confucius wrote, 2,500 years ago, that it is difficult to find anyone who will study for three years without thinking of money. But it is not so simple. Education undertaken solely with a remote, practical end in view can be insufferably dull. It needs to be illuminated at every stage, if only fitfully by the inherent interest that characterizes the pursuit of knowledge. Education is "autotelic"—a self-rewarding occupation. This quality is most clearly demonstrated in the education of young children, but it is persistent in greater or less degree throughout the lives of most people. There is a deep delight in learning that is a profoundly human characteristic. We are constantly in danger of overestimating the purely economic motive. Perhaps we can say that for many people, economic motives lure them into college, and the unsuspected delights of education keep them there.

We see constantly at work the interplay of both motives—the practical and immediate on the one hand, and on the other the importance and fascination of completely disinterested learning, uncontaminated by self-interest or even by practical usefulness.

Curriculums in the so-called liberal arts colleges are heavily infused with subjects having an occupational or professional cast, while schools devoted to professional fields, whether engineering, business, or journalism, find it important that their graduates become immersed in the liberal arts at first hand. It is a curious anomaly that we have been so long in recognizing that both of these elements are essential to education—we have persisted in treating them as mutually exclusive. As Alfred North Whitehead put it: "The antithesis between a technical and a liberal education is fallacious. There can be no adequate technical education which is not liberal, and no liberal education which is not technical; that is no education which does not impart both technique and intellectual vision."[9]

The college, in exhibiting its wares, need not feel ashamed that some programs, even at the undergraduate level, tend toward some definable, useful niche in society. Such an objective, even though it may turn out to be mistaken in direction, imparts to the student an impulse and direction and a certain sturdy self-respect which is hard to reproduce in an atmosphere of completely neutral cognition. So it is only natural that the great majority of college undergraduates today should be in programs that have a definable occupational objective, or at least an occupational tendency. Thus the demand side of the talent equation feeds back continually into the supply, shifting its direction and emphasis. This feedback sometimes follows too closely the ephemeral fluctuations in the job markets. But basically, the job market in its broad tendencies must be followed.

Another complicated set of social forces comes into play here: social mobility and the desire for it, parental ambition, customary levels of aspiration, regional and ethnic groupings with special objectives. Such influences impinge on the admissions process, affecting the demand for education, the direction it takes, and the way it affects individual colleges.

These, then, are some of the social complexities with which the problem of college admissions is entangled. In an earlier era, preoccupation with the academic hurdles erected to control entrance led to almost complete neglect of the deeper, social forces which in reality determined who entered college. Contemporary admissions problems usually present themselves to the admissions committee or the admissions officer in terms of the recruiting-cum-selection complex. Detailed academic qualifications in terms of subject-matter definitions have receded in importance; considerations of aptitude and achievement as measured by marks and tests have come to the fore. But with this evolution, there is still a general neglect of the deeper cultural and social forces at work. To understand his job, the admissions officer or the faculty member concerned with admissions needs some understanding of the place of his efforts in this social process.

## Scarcity and Selection

The most conspicuous feature of higher education in the world today is the universal and growing shortage of facilities in relation to the demand for education.[10] Every nation in the world is seeking to multiply and enlarge its universities. Some, especially among the developing countries, are doing this in an atmosphere of total emergency and crash programs. In many others cost, apathy, habit, and the vested interests and inertia of an ancient establishment impose such a lag that the gap between demand and supply, instead of shrinking, widens from year to year. The unslaked thirst for education is building up, in entire populations, pressures that may well topple governments in the years ahead.

The people most in demand in modern society are the kinds turned out by universities, even universities in their current version, often unregenerate, unreconstructed, and complacent. Such harmless foibles as medieval regalia are too often accompanied by medieval habits of thought. So the emergency can easily cause faculties and administrations to remain smug. If one is so sought after, it is easy to conclude that all one's works are superlatively good. The valid concept of "high standards" gets shifted from an honest ideal of effective teaching and scholarship to the unlimited, negative principle of exclusion. If Satan tempts the professor, it is in offering him an opportunity to eliminate all but the ablest 10 percent—or 1 percent—of potential students. Then he can enjoy to the full the luxury of being exemplar, guide, and mentor of the surviving remnant of devoted and brilliant disciples, and yet have a good conscience, since it is all done in the name of high standards. He has a defense, although he may have added immensely to the "human scrap piles." This is not to say by any means that all students are fitted for the more exacting kinds of higher education. There will always be a difficult problem of differentiation and classification. The point is that scholars of the utmost integrity and the highest ideals can, by the very fact of their high standards, be diverted from the underlying social obligation to provide education by the assertion of a kind of divine right of exclusion.

The tidal wave of demand for university-educated people is due not only to the advance in science and technology, but more broadly to the need for specialists in every field, and the protean growth of expert specialisms throughout society. The intellectual component of the work of the world is rapidly crowding out not only the muscular components but also the habitual and unthinking components that could formerly, without undue penalty, be ignorant as well. These are forces that generate a powerful demand for education. They are reinforced, too, by needs even more profound than the need for expert specialisms. The complexity and interdependence of today's close-knit and shrinking world demand that all judgments and decisions be made in the light of a degree of intelligence and maturity never to be found in an ignorant populace. Along with multiplied needs for expertise of all kinds goes the necessity for informed and balanced judgment reaching across the boundaries of special disciplines. Thought liberated by education must be harnessed to meet imperative human and social emergencies.

The lag that slows the higher educational establishment in its expansion is due to another set of forces, also social in a broad sense.

These are partly fiscal; the costs of expansion are enormous even though they are in reality investments rather than expenditures. Part are due to the class structure of old societies, to traditional thought habits, sometimes to poorly organized secondary school systems. Part, too, are due to vested interests and inertia within the older universities. The unexamined dogma that "more means worse" has been for generations a refuge for vested interests in the status quo. It is now in the process of being rapidly eroded, if not indeed contradicted. Whatever the causes, the lag exists and is traceable to many kinds of social disequilibrium. So we return to the fundamental conclusion that, seen in worldwide perspective, access to higher education, whatever its intellectual trappings, its nominal standards, is regulated in greater or less measure by social forces having at most only a limited effectiveness in identifying and nurturing the ablest.

Meanwhile the result is an emphasis on selection that is acute and unavoidable. This imbalance is, in the longer view, a transitional situation; in its excessive form it is undesirable and to be tolerated only as an emergency condition. Under any reasonable conditions of equilibrium between supply and demand, selection could be less drastic. The underlying obligation to provide education would override the privilege of a selection that in some countries and some universities is procrustean beyond reason. Most of the applicants refused access to higher education under these acute conditions—much worse in some other countries than here—have the ability to profit by and should be admitted to some variant form of it.

In many nations the running disparity between the demand and supply of education has led to drastic, even heroic, screening measures. These may consist of examinations or other hurdles that are intellectual in form but do not effectively identify the ablest. They may be based, for example, on an obsolete syllabus; they may reward rote memory, or the reflection of received opinion, or persistence in taking tests, rather than intellectual power. Such hurdles reduce numbers without insuring that those showing the greatest promise should be chosen for admission. Populations have often showed remarkable patience with situations involving unreasonable or misdirected selectivity, perhaps because they have regarded universities with awe born of ignorance. There are signs that this patience may be running out.

For most colleges in the United States recruiting and selection go on concurrently, one or the other being more emphasized as conditions change. It is a kind of paradox that many of the most selective colleges carry on the most vigorous recruiting. The naive view that selection and recruiting are alternatives—that one recruits when he needs more students, and selects when he needs fewer—is so over-simplified as to be quite misleading. Every college, however low its standards, will refuse some applicants, and conversely, even the most sought-after college will bestir itself to attract candidates whom it regards as exceptional.

But these are practical, surface phenomena. The selection principle raises deeper social and educational issues about which most people have strong views but little real knowledge. Each college is busy selecting among applicants—some very vigorously select a minority of applicants in, others rather loosely select a minority out. In every case concepts are entertained of comparative merit, worth, or promise. We don't know how far these are valid or absolute, or how far they reflect predispositions and prejudices built into us by the culture in which we are imbedded or by the subculture in which we grew up. Least of all can we be sure whether these very unconscious and unrecognized predispositions may not be shutting off, perversely and tragically, types of talent that we simply have not learned to recognize or to encourage. One has only to read at random in the field of biography to realize that the history of education is strewn with unrecognized talent. All admissions officers and admissions committees share in this general ignorance. The college justifies its selectivity on two main grounds: first, it says, the intellectual issues and processes with which it deals are esoteric, erudite, subtle. They can be dealt with adequately only by students of more than average intellectual power and stature; we have assembled a faculty of great distinction, whose efforts would be wasted on the mediocre. This argument is especially persuasive in the natural sciences, where a student without the necessary aptitude and preparation, particularly in mathematics, quickly sinks without a trace.

Second, argues the college, we are going to be judged, in the last analysis, by the broad effectiveness of our graduates in the context of society. We are entitled to pick the people that seem most likely to contribute the most value and will have the maximum impact on the life of their time.

These are defensible arguments, but they nevertheless often serve as rationalizations for a kind of insensate avarice: we want the best and only the best, we are never satisfied, we regret that every class, no matter how able and promising, still has a bottom third. There are some professors who can never quite reconcile themselves to the fact that some students are better than others. If we could only chloroform all but the top 1 percent, how ideal the world would be! Yet this is not merely a form of human avarice. It is also deeply connected with the highest virtues of the academic man—the impulse toward perfection. What looks like greed is the obverse of idealism, and of a dedicated search for excellence. Under these conditions it is easy for selection to become, to a degree, a substitute for education. A student body so outstanding in its talents that it shines under any kind of educational process may have the effect of reducing the motivation for improving that process. Every professor wants disciples. If a good supply of them, able and eager, is deposited annually at his door, he need give little thought to improving the quality of the educational process as he himself embodies it.

Granted, for the sake of argument, that selective colleges know what they are about, that they really succeed in picking the ablest and most promising youth coming forward year by year, what would happen if every college did the same? In a later chapter in this book there is presented a theoretical model in which a hierarchy of colleges, ranked from the most sought after to the least sought after, accepts and rejects in a manner which results in the ablest students frequenting the strongest colleges, and the least promising students sifting downward into the weakest colleges. One must grant that some tendency does exist toward the evolution of such a model. But it seems certain that the forces tending to scatter talent widely and to bring it to fruition in the most odd and unexpected places will continue to be dominant. It has not by any means been demonstrated that the overall welfare of the nation or of humanity at large would best be served by concentrating all the ablest students in a few of the strongest universities.[11]

The problems are not so simple as this model suggests. We don't really know which are the "best" students, or even whether the "best" colleges are doing nearly as good a job as they might. If the White House is to be occupied in one year by a graduate of Harvard and in the next by a graduate of Southwest Texas Teachers' College (an institution which, however great its merits, has less *réclame*, and less power to attract students from a distance), then both colleges had better be good.

In the broad context of the general welfare, the overwhelming obligation of higher education is the provision of education for all capable of realizing its benefits and feeding these back in multiplied vigor into the general polity. Seen in this wide context, the selection versus rejection problem is converted into one of differentiation, classification, multiple characterization. No doubt it will become more apparent in the years to come how far it is necessary or desirable to differentiate higher education into environments of widely different kinds with reference to such characteristics as degrees of intellectual sophistication, practical versus theoretical bent, or social involvement versus detachment. It may even be possible to find out how to "fit" each student into a college with an atmosphere—social, moral, intellectual—whose tone evokes from him the most active response. All this remains at the borderline of human knowledge, though enough experimentation has been carried on to suggest that some progress can be made.

For the foreseeable future things will remain pretty chaotic. It is realistic therefore to define the basic view of the admissions process as the result of a series of social forces, often blind, seldom fully understood, interacting in complex ways. Reason enters into this process, but only fitfully and partially. Devices such as school grades and marks, clumsy at best, do serve a helpful purpose. Tests, after a half-century of development, have proved to be useful adjuncts in the general classification process. But they are easily misused; and critics who want to abolish tests forget that it is usually some obvious misuse of this valuable device, and not testing itself, that leads to trouble.

If the individual college sees its fundamental public obligation for providing education chiefly in the guise of a right to select ever more rigorously, the result must be defensible on some grounds broader than a blind, avaricious impulse to reach out for more and better. Leaving aside the delicate question whether College A deserves better students, or whether it has done anything to earn them (except for high-pressure recruiting), there remain many other unanswered questions. Do the "best" colleges indeed attract the best (or most) students? Are some colleges merely marshaling yards for switching groups of students from particular secondary schools with particular clienteles, reshuffling and sorting them, and moving them on into various postgraduate destinations? May this traffic-interchange function overshadow the educational process itself, so that the institution becomes a kind of large-scale broker in talent, rather than a generator of education in its own right?

To ask questions of this kind is to present a series of caricatures, necessarily exaggerated, yet pointing to tendencies that are to some extent present and operative in the contemporary scene. The individual student is so intent on gaining admission to some college he regards as suitable that he takes the existing situation quite as it is. He has neither time nor inclination for critical analysis. The system, with all its inherent chaos and unreason, is nevertheless a built-in part of his problem, and he has to cope with it as it is. The extensive literature on "how to get into college," much of it very good and very useful, is pitched to this situation. It is uncritical in the sense of accepting the educational world as it is, and helping the student get his bearings in it.

The individual college, as well, has a struggle and its own set of problems to meet, financial and otherwise. It is intent on getting more students, or better students (by its own quite uncertain definition), or some combination of the two. Its standards of excellence in selecting students are a complex mixture of values derived from the faculty, the administration, the alumni, the community, the coaching staff, and the surrounding culture. In this way, the college is as intent on its own problem and as self-centered as is the harassed student.

Both are running a maze whose exits and goals are partly hidden from them. Seldom indeed is a serious effort made to get a bird's-eye view of the process with the general welfare as the ultimate criterion. Yet to make a serious effort in this direction is a first duty of any admissions officer or admissions committee seeking a broad perspective on its task.

## Levels of Analysis

The three chapters that follow are organized around the concept of three standpoints from which the general problem of access to education can be viewed. They will be focused mainly on conditions in the United States. The first viewpoint is that of the individual student, or Level One; the second that of the individual college, or Level Two. The third, or Level Three, presents a conspectus of the system as a whole, including the competitive and cooperative relationship among all colleges in the matter of the entrance and exit of students.

These are not merely three viewpoints chosen at random; they are organically related in a hierarchy of degrees of complexity. They can properly be regarded not only as three modes of discourse, but even more appropriately as three levels of analysis at progressively higher degrees of complexity. The process remains the same, but the purview of the discussion broadens, and the intricacy of the analysis increases, from level to level.

Level One is clearly the simplest. Guidance counselors, parents, teachers, and other advisers seeking to help the student fall into this level of discussion, often quite unconsciously. The extensive literature on how to choose a college, or how to get into college, is carried on strictly at this level.[12]

Level Two concerns only the single college, but the problems of a single college are manifold and difficult, with many conflicts of principle and difficult choices. Level Two is a higher plane of complexity. Most of the professional literature on admissions is written, again quite unconsciously, on this level. The existence of other colleges is ignored, except as they may appear as competitors, or rarely, as models. The inevitable article that the admissions officer writes at intervals for the alumni magazine is Level Two discourse, pure and un-defiled. The dominant criterion against which everything is judged is the interest, or supposed interest, of the single college, its image and aggrandizement. The unspoken assumption is that what is good for College X is good for the United States.

The tacit presupposition is that the college seeks, and should have, more students, or "better" students, or both. Such questions as whether the college deserves more or better students, or whether some of its students might better, in their own interest and in the public interest, go to college elsewhere, lie outside the purview of this body of thought. The typical admissions committee, like the faculty and the administration it represents, is, in the candid phrase of one such committee, "greedy" for talent.[13] Colleges are generally quite willing to tell the applicant, "You are not good enough for us." Few ever say "We are not good enough for you."

Level Three is the "systems" view of the entire process, and so is at a still higher degree of complexity. Discussion at this level involves the interaction of all the colleges and universities with each other and with secondary schools, as they appraise and deliver their annual crop of students coming forward out of the society; it involves not only the "manpower" demands of the economy in a narrow sense, but also the demands of the entire polity for an increasingly literate society, an increasingly knowledgeable electorate, and a citizenry with a depth of cultural awareness that would scarcely have been thought of a generation ago. At Level Three it is permissible, at least, to query whether what College X thinks is good for it is indeed good for the United States and in the public interest.

"The great sorting" between high school and college is referred to here as a social process. In discussion or analysis conducted at Level Three, this process is regarded as a whole, rather than from the single viewpoint of the student, or the self-regarding stance of the college, with its own problems of growth and survival. The forces involved in the system as a whole are the same as those involved in the sorting process, but many of them are not directly visible to the student. The competition between colleges, the play of economic demand for talent, the fluctuations of the manpower market, all form a part of the system as looked at on Level Three. Thus the "systems" view is the analytical view of the social process of sorting, followed back to its roots in both the supply and the demand for talent.

This essay, then, is directed especially to school guidance people whose natural idiom of discourse is at Level One, and admissions officers whose habits of thought are necessarily focused on problems at Level Two, in the hope that by looking more broadly at the system as a whole, that is by thinking at Level Three, they may gain in perspective on their own professional problems.

# 2. The Student and His Future

## Focus of Decision

At Level One, that of the individual student, the "system" with its constituent structure of schools and colleges is taken for granted as it stands. Whatever its defects, injustices, or illogicalities, it is there; the student has to deal with it if he is to find and enter a college. To the extent that the high school teacher or guidance counselor identifies himself with the student's problem—and he typically does this— he functions also at this level.

There is an extensive literature on the theme of "choosing a college," or "how to get into college." This literature has special importance for students in the United States who have open to them a bewildering variety of educational opportunities. Yet, in any broad sense, it has to be uncritical, accepting the complexities and idiosyncrasies of higher education in the United States as "given." Matters of history, evolution, change, or reform are beyond its scope, as are normative views of what higher education "ought" to be. It is "ad hoc," and its end is served once the student gets into a college. He is then assumed to have solved his educational problem, at least passably.

However complex the social forces that condition the problem of access to college, they must all come to a focus in the mind and intention of the individual student. He, in the last analysis, must decide whether he wants to go to college; and for this decision, whether it is yes or no, he usually produces some colorable reason or rationalization. If the decision is yes, he then has to decide where he wants to go, make some estimate about where he probably can go, and make and implement a series of subsidiary decisions. If, alas, a parent or a counselor makes these decisions for him, the student still has to live with the consequences. On him alone rests the responsibility for making some kind of adjustment to the college environment; he alone can provide the continuing drive and energy necessary to get an education. The world of admissions at Level One shows, in the student's conception, no tendency to change. It is part of his existential environment, scarcely thought of as subject to growth, evolution, or reform. It is "given." His problem is merely to cope with it.

## The Inarticulate Major Premise

What is the student's equipment as he embarks on this task? Most basic of all, and least noticed, is the cultural matrix within which he has been nurtured, which has conditioned his attitudes, beliefs, and expectations. His unconscious sense of what life is about and of the ends of existence goes back to this deep level, but he generally cannot explain or understand it. Anthropologists studying a culture must depend heavily upon "informants" from within the culture. They listen carefully to what the informant says but do not make the easy assumption that the informant knows why he does what he does, or even that he can accurately report what he does. It is assumed, rather, that what people say about what they do and why they do it is itself the product of a system of beliefs provided by the culture and forming an integral part of it. "The total configuration of belief and patterned behavior characterizing a society is infinitely more complex than any participant can understand, and perhaps even more complex than the relatively detached and intellectually objective observer can understand."[14] The individual nurtured in a culture has its received opinions built into him, and they become his own, a part of his personality structure; he wants to act in ways that the cultural pattern of beliefs requires that he should act. He is characteristically unconscious of the source of his attitudes. They have been absorbed to such an extent that he is convinced either that they are self-evident or that he has thought them up unaided. We are all to some extent brainwashed by our environment.

This basic principle of cultural anthropology should make us exceedingly wary in interpreting any data derived by asking people "why" they do anything. Questions directed to students about why they want to go to college, or did or did not go to college, or chose a particular college, tell a great deal about the patterns of belief that prevail in our culture but relatively little about the inner motivations of the students themselves.

Much as the basic endowment of attitudes and beliefs differs from person to person depending on individual origins, there is a common core, least visible of all, because it is so nearly all-pervasive. Like the "receptacle" in Plato's thought, this is the ground of being which conditions all particulars, the "foster mother of all becoming," the background, sensed rather than seen, against which all diversity and change are perceived.[15] These form "the inarticulate major premise" of our thinking, "the things we know but cannot tell." At the deepest level, the major premise derives from our common humanity and forms the permanent base on which rest all the less fundamental elements of culture that are relative and changeable to such a great extent from one people to another. This underlying common denominator includes the existence of two sexes, the fact that all men are mortal, that all need food and shelter, that all must communicate, and can have no real personal existence except through relationships with others, that all crave affection, and that many are quarrelsome.

## The Cultural Matrix

In contemporary American society, we should find among the unanalyzed presuppositions of the attitudes and beliefs held by the majority of students, vestiges of many concepts that have come down through the centuries in the western world. The Judeo-Christian monotheistic background is powerful, often felt rather than consciously attended to. The ideas of John Locke and of the eighteenth-century enlightenment are closely interwoven with our governmental theory and with popular ideas of it. There are important traces of uncritical nineteenth-century optimism and its characteristic belief in progress. There are veins and deposits of Calvinist inner-directedness (in David Riesman's phrase), all characteristic of earlier stages of our development. Strong remnants persist of that restless, energetic individualism, that impatience with the doctrinaire and theoretical, and that bent for the practical, that grew up as a natural adaptation to the challenge of the frontier and the westward expansion. The Horatio Alger spirit is certainly far from dead in our national ethos.

Elements such as these are legacies from a past now rapidly receding. The contemporary structure of beliefs shows many signs of adaptation to an environment which, despite islands of poverty, is the most opulent the world has ever known. The basic principle of the welfare state has come to be widely accepted within little more than a generation. The growing governmental sector is still small compared with the area of free enterprise. It is a society predominantly industrial and commercial; agriculture has rapidly shrunk in percentage terms and now occupies only a small minority of the working population. The service industries are correspondingly expanding. The society's concentration into large urban areas is an irrestible force with which we have not yet learned how to deal. Widely prevalent too, among youth, are the kinds of expectations and beliefs that accompany a relatively fluid society still characterized by high social mobility. Class distinctions are conspicuous but have not acquired the caste-like rigidity so typical of older cultures in which they often came to be regarded as unalterable facts of nature.

It is a society that is physically mobile as well. The movement of population among states generates a constant stirring and mixing that weakens regionalism, whether of dress, accent, or attitude. This homogenization is accentuated by the mass media of communication which, despite their primary dedication to commerce via entertainment, perform an important educational function. The average high school youngster has a social awareness and sophistication far beyond that of a generation ago, even though the sophistication is partly superficial, and the awareness less than complete. These are powerful counterforces to the built-in centrifugal tendencies of a society as diverse and pluralistic as ours. Even the tightest and most insulated subcultures find their ghettos of isolation more and more invaded and interconnected by unifying tendencies. These then, impressionistically sketched, are some of the components in the climate of opinion and attitude in which the student is immersed.

In this matrix there are dark areas—disadvantaged minorities of which the Negro population is the most conspicuous. Puerto Ricans, Mexican-Americans, Indians, and a large group not identifiable by color or national origin who are trapped in pockets of poverty, not only in Appalachia but in many other places, share, in their own special ways, the same general sorts of disabilities and handicaps. For a youngster in one of these groups the controlling background of attitude and motive is far different from that of the majority. The structure of personality is different, and the whole approach to education must therefore be different. As noted previously, the extent to which these adverse influences can be countered by timely educational intervention is one of the key discoveries of this century.

The matrix of inherited basic attitude is constantly infiltrated by the prevailing values of the surrounding culture. Young people are immersed in a world of advertising, bombarded with claims that they soon learn are mostly exaggerated and may therefore be automatically discounted. The inevitable result of exposure to this barrage is a healthy skepticism which may be counted as a positive, if unintended, result of modern advertising. The phenomenon of "brand loyalty," often a product of this bombardment, is also a form of defense against it. One is reminded of Alfred North Whitehead's remark that a creed, itself a product of speculation, is also a device for limiting speculation. The customer, having gained from whatever source some impression of reputation and familiarity for a product, clings to the brand name for security's sake. It is not accidental that pecking orders of "prestige" among colleges should have grown up and received a considerable recognition in a society conditioned to associate quality with reiterated brand names and slogans. Universities of illustrious name and worldwide repute have existed since the Middle Ages, but in the United States the special problem exists of distinctions among immense numbers of institutions in a situation in which the student has an extremely wide range of choice and of substitution, and very inadequate means of making truly informed or realistic, comparative judgments. David Riesman and others have advocated a kind of "consumers' research" effort to inform students about colleges. It is uncertain whether this might offset the already exaggerated effort to find the "best" college.[16]

Among the most important elements in the student's background of attitude and belief is the rapidly growing belief in the importance of education. This extends through all elements of society and is, indeed, a worldwide phenomenon. Closely joined to the "revolution of rising expectations" now universal in almost all nations is the conviction that education is the chief instrument by which rising expectations can be fulfilled. The need of governments for trained manpower exerts a strong upward pull to draw youth into higher education—a pull reinforced even more powerfully from below by the desire of young people to better themselves. This conviction is at the root of the rapid and persistent growth of the proportion of the age group seeking to enter college in the United States. It is held not only by those highly motivated toward higher education, but also by those who, often regretfully, decide that it is not for them. Conversely, the characteristic nineteenth-century distrust of higher education as a "frill" is rapidly weakening even among those who do not regard themselves as destined for it.[17]

Elements such as these, differing from person to person, and from one subculture to another, make up the background cultural matrix of ideas lying deep in the mind of the student as he gradually awakens to his social surroundings—the backdrop against which the drama is played. But in the foreground, as active protagonists, are two major forces that condition his entire educational progress. These are on the one hand the spontaneous desire to learn and on the other the practical need to get ahead, to hold a job, to gain a marketable skill, to better oneself in the world.

## The Useful and the Poetic

This contrast is in part the contrast between the ideal and the practical—or more precisely, between the poetic (in the widest sense of the word) and the utilitarian. But even this does not convey the full sense; for the desire to learn has deep biological roots and carries survival value. This innate pleasure in using the mind expresses a profound need of the organism, and it becomes numbed and paralyzed only under special conditions.

Education at the earliest levels is almost entirely spontaneous—even unconscious, as when the child learns to talk and grasps some elementary rules of social behavior. This same spontaneous joy in learning, in mastering some increasingly intricate code or system of symbols and ideas is utilized in the current movement to carry young children much further than before into such fields as mathematics and science. The key is to encourage situations in which the child discovers principles for himself.[18] By postponing somewhat the authoritative imposition of rote learning, it is possible also to postpone at least for a time the stage when the child begins to be presented with "inert ideas" (in A. N. Whitehead's expressive phrase); his eye begins to glaze over, and he loses the first spontaneous enthusiasm.

The improvements that have taken place in education in our generation have significantly extended the period during which this spontaneous pleasure in learning can be maintained and have increased the proportion of students moved by this wellspring of interest. But at the higher levels, prudential considerations inevitably take command.

Most higher education involves a tension between these two polar opposites. There are, at one extreme, a few "natural students" for whom the urge to know is overmastering, who need no other incentive. At the other extreme is the much larger group impelled by practical considerations to "hire themselves educated." For these, a degree is the goal, and what pleasure and interest can be got along the way is only a small extra. The great bulk lie between these extremes, the useful and the poetic. Without some spark of response to the inherent interest of the subject, study becomes so intolerably dull that few could continue it; some vestige of interest in learning is always present in those who stick to a course. To help them over the dull stretches, there is the shining hope of a degree and a job.

Of these dual forces, it seems clear that at the stage of admission to college the prudential is the more powerful. In our culture, it is a psychological necessity for most students to have at least a tentative occupational goal of some kind by the time they enter college. This need is apparent from the large majority who enter four-year programs nominally directed at such fields as business, journalism, nursing, engineering, or "premedical." Even the minority who enter a nominally undifferentiated "liberal arts" course include a substantial group whose actual orientation is vocational, as expressed for example by a chemistry or economics major. At the same time, the proportion of genuine liberal arts studies included in the nominally vocational courses is steadily rising. The undifferentiated liberal arts programs tend to attract a larger proportion of "natural students," for whom eventual graduate study is a natural sequel, and also a larger proportion of those sufficiently well-to-do to be able to extend the exploratory period preceding an occupational commitment. For this fortunate few, the undergraduate years of "moratorium" can be a ripening period of great value. These contrasting motives, seen against the backdrop of innate cultural predisposition, are the key factors in the decision to continue education past the secondary level, and to a large extent also the key to the choice of a college.

These influences bear upon the student as he begins in a conscious and purposeful way to think about whether to continue his education after high school, and where. In the last two high school years he begins to play a major part in "the great sorting." Under the special conditions that obtain in the United States, a great deal of conscious choice has to be exercised by individual students, but many extraneous influences intervene to affect this choice, for better or worse.

The exuberant, even chaotic variety of colleges and universities in the United States is a potential asset of incalculable value. Free enterprise and initiative function in parallel with state-operated education. The history of weak denominational colleges throughout the nineteenth century has led into a situation in which public higher education increasingly shoulders the main burden but privately sponsored institutions serve as a source of innovation, variety, and experiment. Many of the privately sponsored colleges of the earlier era have evolved into universities of high standards of excellence. These are pacesetters; only the strongest state universities equal them. The small, independent colleges of the nineteenth century carried a double burden: sectarian narrowness and rivalry, which almost automatically eliminated itself within a generation or two; and a pedantic, narrow version of the classical curriculum, which had to give way before the broader educational needs of the time. Natural selection eliminated many of these institutions; most of the survivors maintained themselves by broadening their appeal.

## Kinds of Intervention

The present situation has one serious disadvantage for the student at Level One: he becomes so caught up in the processes of choice, selection, comparison, and competitive differences among colleges that he loses sight of the main issue, the educational process itself. He is encouraged to think of education as something favorable that will be done to him, or in his behalf. Attainment of membership among the happy few seems a final goal rather than a beginning. So the task of guidance, from whatever source, is to emphasize to the student the central importance of his own initiative. He must learn to see the college as an incidental aid and supplement to his own effort, not as the source from which all enlightenment streams down. College, to change the metaphor, is a crutch, not a stretcher. Having grasped this concept, he is still faced with the necessity for choice and the tactical problem of implementing it.

In a wholly rational world, the student would look to the stated purpose of a college to determine whether it might meet his needs. Up to a certain point, catalog information will serve him as a useful guide to its curricular orientation. But to draw up a general statement of a college's purpose is a task, deceptively simple in appearance, which has defeated most authors of catalog prose.[19] Such statements are likely to have little practical bearing on the processes involved in "the great sorting." Naive efforts to state in simple, straightforward terms the objectives of a school or college are seldom successful. Education is, above all, an open-ended process. A great many things, fortunately, happen to students that neither they nor anyone else had planned or contemplated. This fact lends a certain air of unreality to any statement about the college's purpose.

For the basic, hard core of simple factual information about colleges, the various standard directories provide help. Though they list more colleges than the student can possibly take account of, they provide perspective on the entire field.

Second, and of greater import in the actual sorting process, are the spheres of influence, the clienteles of patronage and association that to a greater or less degree cling to and encircle each institution. For denominational colleges, or those with a history of denominational support, these spheres of interest are likely to lie largely within the membership of a church group. Beyond this circle, in all colleges, lies the sedulously cultivated group of alumni and parents, with all the points of social radiation such a group inevitably sets up. Such influences constitute a major and active form of intervention in the sorting process, and the individual student is frequently caught up in them and swept into a particular college before he knows it.

Third, there is always a powerful geographical force that tends to make higher education predominantly a local business; the sphere of influence of any school or college is likely to be strongest within a small geographical radius of the institution itself. As demonstrated in the last section of this book, "College Admissions as a System," propinquity is probably the most powerful single influence on college selection. Barriers erected against nonresidents by state institutions, regrettable on educational grounds, have increased as admissions pressures have grown and have lessened geographical diversification. The full impact of propinquity on educational opportunity, however, may be seen in California which is dotted with more than 70 two-year community colleges that have free tuition. Virtually every resident has one of these community colleges within driving distance. Granted that in this context the student misses certain values of the residential college, it may still be that the undiluted influence of the educational process itself is seen here, shorn of the false glamour of the "collegiate" tradition. It has taken the United States several centuries to move into educational concepts broader than the European tradition of students as a small, favored, and sheltered group, somewhat artificially segregated from the surrounding culture and enjoying special privileges. The commuting student and the adult student contribute other values and may develop attitudes that can make more natural the lifelong addiction to continued learning that the conditions of the age require.

Fourth, intervention includes activities directed specifically at recruiting, in the sense of a direct effort by the college to interest and attract students for the ensuing year. Such activities shade off gradually into long-range public relations programs, with legitimate guidance of students as their main object, and mutual communication between college and secondary school as their main instrument. Publications, bulletins, school visits, college conferences and the like, the importing of students and of school representatives for campus visits—all, in greater or less degree, contribute to this overt attempt to inform and attract those who are thought to be peculiarly well qualified as potential students. In all this activity, there is a mixture of propagandist effort on behalf of individual colleges and guidance of a broader sort that has to do with categories of institutions and the realms of value inherent in the world of higher education. The student, though conscious that he is being wooed, cannot help acquiring some sense of what the educational process is about.

Fifth, and most specific of the overt means of intervention, are the direct financial aids offered to students. The categories of student excellence that are thought to merit financial aid are widely varying in different institutions. But it is essential to distinguish between aids awarded for the exercise of specific talents (athletic, musical, or what not) and aids extended in recognition of broad qualities of character and intellect such as will come later to fruition. Financial aids of the former kind tend in one way or another to exploit the student for the benefit of the institution, or to further some end thought to deserve special support apart from the objective of educating him. In student aid of the latter type, an estimate of the ultimate contribution of the student to society is the final criterion, and a compelling case can be made for the view that this is the only justifiable basis for financial aid. The really difficult problems in allocating such grants arise not out of any disagreement on this point, but out of the difficulty of predicting in advance which qualities are in fact likely to be most fruitful, and how "need" should enter the equation.

Sixth, the colleges intervene in the sorting process by interposing a direct veto on a certain number of applicants. This veto may range all the way from a minimum standard of academic achievement, which screens out a few clearly unqualified candidates, to a competitive situation in which only the strongest candidates are taken, and many who are well qualified are turned away because of lack of space. Taking the college world as a whole, this is a less important kind of intervention than public opinion supposes it to be. While to some extent colleges select students (and even the least selective college does some selecting), to a much greater extent, in this country, students select colleges. Even the high-standard college upholds its quality not so much by rejecting applicants as by establishing a reputation that attracts many able and ambitious students and, in the main, scares away the weaker ones. In other words, preselection of the college by the student, even in this era of selective admissions, is more important than screening of students by the college. The colleges probably intervene in the sorting process less than they suppose themselves to, and to the extent that they do intervene, it is often their reputations rather than their actions that are the effective agencies of intervention. The college "telegraphs its punches" by making known its standards and preferences. Potential applicants take these into account. Guidance counselors in the high schools anticipate college action by steering elsewhere those likely to be marginal.

Seventh, the colleges intervene by announcing formal "entrance requirements," in terms of required years of study of specific subjects. As already pointed out, the tendency in recent years has been to reduce this kind of requirement to a bare minimum. The colleges are discovering that when most of their applicants are firmly grounded in secondary education, they can devote their energies to selecting students on broad grounds of character and intellect. How far this effort is successful is problematical. In any case it is a complete reversal of the earlier policy of insisting on specified preparatory subjects in combinations that were often difficult to defend except on grounds of tradition and precedent. It is in the area of accumulative knowledge, particularly in mathematics and science, that the strongest case can be made for specific subject-matter requirements.

These are some of the cross currents among which the student must navigate. Where, among this welter of influences, does educational guidance belong? If the guidance counselor is to avoid authoritative direction and indoctrination, he has to act as a kind of alter ego of the student himself—more experienced, with a broader perspective and more special knowledge, but dedicated above all to the student's best interests. This position imposes on him the imperative, within the limits of his vision, to make available to the student such wisdom as he can muster, to convey to him some sense of the contingent and probabilistic nature of the relevant information and of the difficulty of arriving at clear-cut decisions free of any risk, ambiguity, or doubt. His task is to exert his influence on the student to keep open as many doors as possible for as long as possible, and to avoid relatively irreversible curricular decisions which may effectively cut off the possibility of college. He cannot change all the students' systems of values, nor can he extend a guarantee against mistakes, though he may cause them to be fewer and less grave in their effects.

The range of quality open to a student is wide, the range of aims and intellectual climates even wider. The baffled student, bewildered in a college that he is not really up to, and the bored student trapped in a college not really up to him, both represent educational waste. Not only, then, is there a formidable information problem, but it is social in its origins. The student may not know what information he needs, or how to get the information he wants, or how to use the information he has.[20] Intelligent educational guidance can help, but many competing sources of information intervene in the crucial decisions. The communication network, taken as a whole, constitutes a major dimension of the broad social problem of access to higher education. In so far as communication lapses, the student has recourse to choice on conventional grounds—propinquity, hearsay, "prestige," fashion, parental association, or chance rumor and advice. All these sources are more social than educational in origin.

That mismatching of student and college under these conditions is not always as serious as it might be is traceable to three reasons: first, the natural resilience and adaptability of youth is such that most boys and girls who fail to reach the "college of their choice" nevertheless turn out to be quite happy in some alternative environment; second, over fairly wide limits, the important educational outcomes depend less on where a student goes to college than on what he does when he gets there; and third, there is an important element of chance that determines what particular confreres and teachers each individual happens to be thrown with. The effects of these particular and randomly determined encounters, for some students, may outweigh the more general atmosphere and character of the college as a whole.

## Education as a Cultural Complex

In guidance literature, the heavy emphasis on the psychology of the individual student, whether in a clinical context or in the actuarial use of test and measurement as aids to guidance, has partially obscured what may be called the cultural anthropology of the guidance function. The counselor should have a deep understanding of the various subcultures from which his students spring and a grasp of their value systems. Too often he has himself represented a middle-class culture which is held out as the sole norm, to the great disadvantage of talented students from minority or deprived environments. He needs a sensitive comprehension of the ethos of the various subcultures from which students come and of the occupational goals and evaluations that move parents and students. He needs a grasp of the world of work in relation both to education and to the forces of parental ambition, misguided or well founded. Scores and marks of any kind, useful as they may be, are measurements of slices cut out of complex cultural configurations. Numbers gain their full meaning only as they aid in describing the cultural complex in which the student is embedded.

It is customary to say that the world of learning is universal and cosmopolitan in the sense that it transcends the limits of local and national cultures. Yet this is true only in a relative degree. Not only does the word culture embody the integrated total of the influences of its historical roots—Hebrew, Greek, Arabic, medieval Christian, and scientific—it also becomes identified with particular segments and subcultures in different environments. The youngster from a deprived minority, seeking education, finds he is being asked to adopt a new culture, a culture that he may associate with a particular social class or ethnic group which in his experience may seem alien or threatening. Is there a merely fortuitous resemblance between the attitudes of a governing elite, a managerial class, or a religious leadership, and the attitudes of the scholarly world? For example, the question has presented itself in acute form in the British universities where gifted students from working-class backgrounds sometimes find themselves painfully cut off from the culture of their homes and families through adoption of a body of mores and attitudes characteristic of a university education long confined to the ruling class, so that the apparatus of learning has long since come to reflect its attitudes and values, even its vocabulary. A similar tension arises as traditional societies transform themselves through Western scientific and technical learning.[21]

The search for a "culture-free" test that would be fair to culturally deprived children has proved elusive. Even the earliest stages of preschool education begin to mold the child into the configurations of cultural habit. The entire educational enterprise is a complex of influences to mold both behavior and personality. These influences keep getting entangled and associated with other cultural forces which are only partially educational in purpose and effect. Education becomes associated with religion, with ethnic and nationalistic aims, beliefs and strivings, and with ideas of social class. Snobbery is endemic in the human species. Education has always been a favorite vehicle of snobbishness, as have innumerable other things such as costume, accent, occupation, housing, and diet. As more and higher education becomes virtually indispensable for a large fraction of the population, it becomes important to disentangle the essence of education—its central meaning and value—from these adventitious contaminants. We literally do not know how far this disentangling can go. Education is a partly utilitarian, partly ideal venture. Because these two aspects are never wholly separable, we shall probably continue to see education in many curious combinations with other cultural manifestations. Yet we still recognize some unity in the world of higher education toward which the student seeking to enter college, though often stumbling and in a fog, is being gradually led.

Despite these complications, the world of western learning exhibits a certain universality in its tradition and outlook. This is traceable to its roots in Greek speculative thought, in Roman law, in medieval monkish learning, and most of all to the powerful influence of science and technology. To find examples of education apart from this central stream, we have to look either at primitive societies, or at such highly developed examples as the ancient Chinese literary tradition, the Talmudic tradition of learning, or the universities of the Arabic culture. None of these has attained a similar universality. The very inclination and readiness to undertake higher education imply, however dimly, some acceptance of the values of this encompassing world of learning and an eagerness to participate in it. At least some adumbrations of these values must reach the student and move him, if he is to respond to the opportunities of higher education. He must have a certain cultural attitude, a mental and emotional "set," absorbed unconsciously from the social environment.

## Constriction at the Roots

The Western university tradition has, then, a certain solidarity and uniformity at the top. The values of the scholarly world in all parts of the globe converge in a respect for firsthand knowledge, whether of "sources" or of natural phenomena, for intellectual integrity, for independence and *lehrfreiheit,* for the careful, persuasive methods of reason, the conscientious weighing of evidence, and the obligation as well as the freedom to publish results. Authority, no matter how august, is rebuttable by new evidence duly presented. Useful knowledge, too, has risen to a status formerly reserved for traditional or ceremonial kinds of learning. Despite international and intercultural differences, this cluster of values is dominant throughout the modern world.

But when we look, by contrast, at the roots of the university in the populations out of which they grow, wide local variations appear in social attitudes. Access to university education has been for the most part restricted to a small fraction of the populace. Even where the apparatus of competitive examination seemed to guarantee a career open to talent, it frequently turned out that limitations of custom as well as economic forces, often closely tied to ideas of social class, sharply curtailed access to the secondary education which was the only gateway to higher education.[22]

The "self-fulfilling prophecy" has been operative in every country: the majority, systematically deprived of educational stimulus, were considered to hold little promise of talent. Being cut off for the most part from the influences that nurture latent talent, they evidenced little of it; and this in turn was cited as the reason for diverting most children into a low-grade "workers'" education. The American Negro, a minority, has shared with European working classes, a large majority, the fate of being caught in this self-generating circle of non-opportunity and nondevelopment.

Simon Newcomb, the astronomer, has told in his recollections how, as a poor farm boy in Nova Scotia in the 1850s, "I had indeed gradually formed, from reading, a vague conception of a different kind of world, a world of light, where dwelt people who wrote books and people who knew the men who wrote books—where lived boys who went to college and devoted themselves to learning instead of driving oxen. I longed much to get into this world, but no possibility of doing so presented itself. I had no idea that it would be imbued with sympathy for a boy outside who wanted to learn."[23]

The contemporary version of this problem is more complex but equally poignant. Even in the United States, where nearly universal opportunity is open for secondary education, there are backwaters and eddies in the educational stream. Subcultures of considerable size exist in which education makes no effective connection with the motivation of the student. There are talented youngsters who do not know themselves to be so, or, if they do, have no idea how to develop their talents. They are enveloped in a peer group swayed by other interests and values; for them life seems to hold quite different meanings, threats, and rewards. The "street culture" of their environment is so noisy and powerful that it completely jams the quieter signals that come in from the world of education. If these signals do indeed reach them, they still have a financial obstacle to overcome; only if by some remote chance this problem is met can they then start even with the prosperous middle-class youngster. Only at this stage do they then encounter, as he does, the ensuing puzzle of choosing one out of many colleges and universities.

In a century the chief locus of the problem of access to higher education has shifted from remote rural regions to the heart of the great metropolitan areas. It has been well said that today's frontier lies in the cities. A Puerto Rican girl in New York or a Negro boy in South Chicago can be in fact as isolated from educational opportunity as was Simon Newcomb a century ago in remote Nova Scotia.[24] His counterparts of course still exist in rural areas today, but the immense forces of urbanization have produced a far more dangerous and explosive social configuration, confined within a small space and ready to be touched off by the slightest spark.[25]

These perilous forces are at the heart of the college admissions problem in the United States. Compared with them, the problem of the middle-class boy or girl trying to decide where to go to college is relatively mild. Yet this problem, too, is worthy of attention, because so much of the effectiveness of education depends on environmental influences of a subtle, almost invisible kind. The student tends to be thrown back on the somewhat nebulous concept of "prestige" for lack of anything more tangible or more specifically related to the quality of the educational process.

The fashionable current hypothesis is that the best known and most prestigious colleges are in some not very clearly defined way "better." In its crassest form, this is simply the widely held belief that a degree from such a college will give preference in employment or social esteem. At one remove from this is the hypothesis that in such institutions the faculty is abler, the facilities superior, the student body more highly selected, and the quality of the educational process to which the student is exposed consequently better. Within certain limits, this may well be the case. But this view overlooks the possibility, first, that applicant pressure, in the current scarcity conditions, is not a safe measure of a college's real excellence, since none of these institutions is nearly as good as it ought to be, could be, and eventually will be; second, that many if not most other colleges, now less sought after, could be radically improved if the processes of educational innovation and experiment were systematically pursued, followed up, and acted upon.[26]

There is a considerable recent literature of differentiation among colleges with reference to their social, intellectual, and psychological atmospheres—the "press" of the environment upon the student.[27] This has great theoretical interest and even some immediate utility in placing the student in an environment suited to his needs. It has by no means displaced the purely intuitive differentiation based on hearsay and gossip, which is still the main reliance of many students and some guidance counselors. The more theoretical approach raises as many questions as it answers. How far will these techniques "freeze" colleges in particular stereotypes? Is the best education one in which all students tend to resemble each other in values and viewpoint? Is the small "specialty" college more comfortable but less truly educational than a large institution in which contrasting subcultures co-exist and interact?

It seems certain that we have underestimated the extent to which education is itself a phenomenon of acquiring customs, values, systems of belief, and habits of thought in addition to the nominal content of learning itself. The "cultural shock" for a student from an alien environment (either a poverty environment or a foreign culture) can defeat even a youngster of outstanding intellectual gifts unless pains are taken to introduce him gradually to ways he does not know and "signals" he does not recognize or understand.

These are the kinds of problems that present themselves to the student seeking higher education. The forces briefly sketched above may be hidden from him or only partly visible to him. He senses simply a confused world of education that he does not understand, in which he is usually forced to exercise choices and make decisions for which he is ill-equipped. The guidance counselor needs to contribute what enlightenment he can, and the admissions officer has an obligation to look beyond the competitive advancement of the interests of his own college and to serve a broader function as trustee of the student's long-term interests and welfare.

# 3. Admissions within the Walls

## Faculty Viewpoint

The ways in which a college or university organizes itself internally to deal with admissions reflect its attitudes about the meaning and purpose of the admissions function in the life of the institution, the attitudes referred to here as constituting the Level Two view. In these organizational expedients there are not only responses to current opinion and alignments but also many fossilized traces of conditions long past. The admissions function, broadly conceived, concerns the deep roots by means of which higher education in general, and the individual college in particular, tap and draw sustenance from the general population.

Few college people concerned with admissions realize how deep these roots are. The invincibly "collegiocentric" posture so characteristic of most colleges largely inhibits attention to the social roots of the educational enterprise. The college thinks of itself as a little community carrying on certain activities and striving toward certain objectives. Obviously there must be an input of students. The faculty, keenly aware that there are numerous young people who are poorly adapted to the routines and seemingly impervious to the influences that the faculty conceives as constituting education, early develops a bias in favor of those with whom they feel most comfortable. Identify and exclude those "unable to profit" from education—this is the simple and obvious prescription. Thus the recruiting and selective processes come to favor particular subcultures, particular temperaments and personality types and styles of behavior, with a bias toward the student who exhibits eagerness tempered by a generous admixture of docility. The teacher has a deep personal need to feel that he is hand-ing on something both wanted and appreciated. So recruiting and selection, to the extent that they are under faculty influence, are generally slanted, often quite unconsciously, in favor of those whose early background and schooling have already carried them some way toward education, who exhibit the cultural traits with which educators feel most at home. Conversely, those standing in the greatest need of education, including some who have great native ability, are often excluded. One is reminded of the merchant who complained that the bank would let him have a loan only if he could prove that he did not really need a loan.

In the kind of admissions activity spontaneously developed by most colleges a heavy weighting exists in favor of adapting the student body (by suitable recruiting and selection) to the processes of the college. Up to a point this kind of adapting is necessary and proper; whether it is a principle that should operate to the exclusion of the converse— adapting the processes of the college to the student body—is more doubtful. The point is that most colleges take the former view automatically and exclusively. Education, in this view, is defined as what the college has long been doing. Those who do not respond to these influences are thus, by definition, ineducable.

The history of land transportation offers an instructive analogy. For centuries it was taken for granted that the direct and obvious way to attack the problem was to adapt the vehicle to the terrain. The horse, the camel, the travois, the sledge, the cart, wagons with wide wheels and wagons with large wheels, were all tried. Even the automobile was sharply limited in its early stages by the omnipresence of mud. It was only after serious attention was paid to adapting the road to the vehicle, first by the device of rails, then by improved highways, that real progress was made. There are encouraging signs that higher education may be beginning to adapt its processes to the student, instead of choosing students to fit preexisting processes. But the internal organization of admissions, as well as the curriculum itself, still reflects the traditional thinking. In its reliance on concepts of "processing" —of subjecting many individuals to what is essentially uniform treatment—higher education, like education at lower levels, has disregarded or suppressed its greatest asset: the inherent diversity of talents with which nature has endowed individuals. Nature, as Emile Duclaux remarked, loves diversity, but education aims at repressing it.

Because the faculty thinks in terms of particular disciplines and bodies of subject matter, its natural impulse is to lay down rather minute specifications about prerequisites for admission. To the degree that the teacher can be relieved of the burden of working through an elementary introduction to his subject, he can spend time on the more recondite aspects that interest him most and can bring the student closer to the cutting edge of new research and new knowledge where the excitement lies. It is easier and a great deal more fun to teach people who are already three parts educated. Thus the hope recurs in faculty discussion that the student will have at least a "decent" elementary grounding, or a "respectable" foundation. Such words have the ring of modest reasonableness. They are supposed to imply that one is willing to settle for the barest minimum, but that nevertheless there are limits; one cannot teach an ape or a complete barbarian. The definition of what is "decent" or "reasonable" may, of course, include anything one wishes—from spelling to an acquaintance with Hamlet; from arithmetic to the second law of thermodynamics. The phrase "college preparation" embodies the quite unconscious arrogance— indeed an innocent arrogance—of generations of college teachers, immersed in this thinking.

There is a kind of *reductio ad absurdum* lurking behind all such reasoning which tends to admit to education those who need it least and to exclude those for whom the "value added" by education would be greatest. It is obviously essential to exclude those so unprepared that they cannot benefit from instruction at the going level, yet this tendency if left unchecked can focus the educational process on a small and indefinitely diminishing fraction of students.

Thus the impelling force behind the institution of faculty committees on admissions has been the solicitude of faculties for specific regulations about the subject matter that students were expected to have mastered. A great deal of faculty debate is concerned with the minutiae of these regulations. The profound sociological implications of admission to higher education and its attendant problems are quite generally ignored. To require a year of calculus as a prerequisite for admission may look like real progress to the mathematics department, which sees the one student who comes in with this added head start. It does not see the many candidates of equal or greater ultimate promise who will be automatically excluded by a provision of this kind.

An interesting sidelight on the evolution of admissions methods and attitude is provided by Broome's history of admissions requirements in the United States, published in 1903.[28] This is a painstaking, thorough, and scholarly review, beginning from the earliest colonial era. But so preoccupied is Broome with internal organization, and with the detailed rearrangements of traditional and conventional subject matter, that all other values are simply ignored. It never occurred to anyone in that era to look more broadly at the social and economic forces which were the real determinants of admission to college. Such pedantry was the culmination of a long process by which the academic mind had managed to dissociate itself from the living world around it.

The assignment of faculty committees to oversee specified academic functions was rare in the early history of American colleges. Only in the last decade or two of the nineteenth century did the use of such committees become prevalent, perhaps in imitation of German university practice; only in this later stage was admissions included among the functions so supervised. It is not entirely clear how far these groups passed upon individual cases or whether, as seems more probable, they were mainly concerned with such aspects of policy as could be expressed in subject-matter regulations.

The history of the "Committee of Ten,"[29] in the decade that preceded the formation of the College Entrance Examination Board, lends support to the latter emphasis. The chaos that then existed was a man-made chaos of detailed specifications, which were essentially arbitrary in nature. The problem, for the student, was real enough; but it was an artifact of educational rigidity, not a problem inherent in basic social or educational causes. The steps taken by joint action to remedy the situation (including the establishment of the College Entrance Examination Board) were useful on the level at which the problem presented itself but did not touch the deeper dilemmas of access to higher education.

## Admissions Officers Emerge

The practice of designating an administrative officer to concern himself with admissions came later. A scattering of larger universities began appointing such officers in the 1920s, but the practice became prevalent only in the 1930s. It was in this period that the notion of selective admissions and a *numerus clausus* for each entering class began to take hold. The earlier practice of establishing admissions requirements, which defined certain preparatory subject matter, set certain minimum standards either of high school performance or examinations or both; and from that point on, nature took its course. The size of entering classes was a dependent variable—the net result-ant of the total number of applicants minus whatever number were automatically disqualified by the operation of the requirements. Large state institutions, operating of necessity by rule, have adhered most nearly to the latter plan, partly because for them it is important to set impersonal requirements. "Rolling" admissions follows essentially the same principle, with or without some degree of selectivity.

Independent colleges and universities were the first to break this pattern; requirements were still published and maintained, but they became, in effect, a candidate's least significant credential. If the total number of applications exceeded a predetermined size, the right was reserved to select among the qualified candidates in order to hold the entering class down to the target figure. There were, of course, many complications and adjustments. Open or rolling admissions could be limited by setting deadlines and final dates. Minimum academic re-quirements could be conveniently stretched by admitting candidates who held one or more "conditions," later to be removed by processes that ranged all the way from "making up" a year's work (the "pound-of-flesh" approach) to the other extreme of simply wiping out the lapse on the ground that the student had successfully finished the first year (the "forgiveness" approach).

By a paradoxical coincidence, the beginnings of the selective prin-ciple in admissions came during the 1930s at a time when the Depres-sion was drastically reducing the number of applicants to all colleges. It remained an ideal scarcely realized until after World War II. For most institutions, particularly the small, financially struggling liberal arts colleges, many of them just emerging from a sectarian control that severely limited their appeal, the decade 1930-1940 was a time of desperate and anxious recruiting. The top priority need was to find enough cash customers so that the college could remain solvent. The appointment of admissions officers became general in this era, and such people had to be, first of all, salesmen.[30] The faculty committee on admissions typically continued its nominal oversight of (more or less elastic) "requirements," but this was shadow-boxing; the root of the matter lay in the job of attracting students.

As time went on, and recruiting became less urgent, the functions of the admissions officer insensibly broadened. It became evident that a kind of iron curtain had shut off the secondary school system from the world of higher education. Over a generation the pendulum had swung to an extreme in which the high schools of necessity had been led to give main attention to noncollege students. As a result, problems of guidance toward higher education, of curricular articulation, and of contact and information were next seen to be urgent and to need attention. *Pari passu* with the development of college guidance as a quasi-professional activity in the high schools, the admissions function began to develop in a similar manner, and to show at least the faint beginnings of a professional approach.

A kind of mutual improvement process got slowly under way.[31] High school counselors found themselves trying to advise students about attendance at colleges about which the counselors knew next to nothing; a great informational gap needed to be filled. Conversely, many people in college were thrown into admissions work with no professional training for it, and no real knowledge of secondary education and its problems. The full range of educational guidance, it came to be realized, was broad enough to comprehend both these groups. With this realization the internal design of college administrations began to change. Communication between college faculty and schools, mutual visits, even exchange of teachers, gradually increased.[32] The rigid view of admissions as the unyielding application of a series of "yes or no" rules began to yield to a broader understanding of the educational, social, and human aspects of the guidance function. Admissions values in this broad sense of educational guidance began to permeate faculty thinking beyond the narrow confines of admissions committees.

At its lowest and least imaginative level, exchange between high school counselors and admissions people constitutes a kind of brokerage operation. At this level, the job is one of negotiation: the high school counselor tries to make the best possible bargain on behalf of his "client" for admission to a strong college. In an independent school, the student is quite literally a client, and in the eyes of status-conscious parents, a school's reputation may, to an embarrassing degree, depend on its success in getting its graduates into the particular colleges favored by its parent group, an objective often only remotely related to the genuine educational worth of the processes carried on in these colleges, or their suitability for the students concerned.

The counselor, if tempted to "oversell" a candidate, knows that he is always subject to the risk that another year the college will be more wary of his recommendations. The admissions officer in turn has a recruiting problem—or thinks he has. He is looking for the strongest students, or those who in his scheme of values are deemed more "desirable." In such an atmosphere of negotiation it is very easy to fall into a predominantly bargaining habit of thought, losing sight of the fact that both parties to the transaction are in a deeper sense obligated to act as trustees for the student's welfare, and to serve in a fiduciary capacity, giving him the benefit of whatever special skill and experience they can muster. What the student or his parents want, or think they want, may not represent the wisest educational solution. But they have a right to choose. Solutions cannot be imposed on them. It is a task of persuasion and diplomacy to carry them, perhaps, some distance but not all the way toward what seems the best solution. There are no certainties; guidance, like politics, remains the art of the possible.

The admissions officer and his colleagues represent characteristic viewpoints about the aims of education and about methods of attracting and selecting students. The academic world is a subculture in itself. True, it has more windows on the universe than the grocery or hardware business. In its worldwide catholicity and universality, it has dimensions centuries old, awe-inspiring and precious; yet it too has its constraints and parochialisms. Not even academia, with its powerful tradition of detached rationality, can ever get wholly outside the framework of its accustomed thinking. Whoever comments upon this must in turn have his own predilections and prejudices. Yet a conscious effort to transcend both the competitive interests of individual colleges and the characteristic habits of thought of the scholarly world can illuminate the forces affecting the inflow of students. Higher education interacts in many ways with the society that contains it. It is an interaction partly defined and shaped by the ways in which it reaches, attracts, and chooses its students. An institution is to be judged by what it does. To look at actual admissions practices, rather than at what an institution professes these practices to be, is to see alma mater *en déshabillé* and without her make-up.

We speak loosely of the college seeking the kind of candidate for admission that it most values. But various elements in an institution may have quite diverse notions of what constitutes a desirable candidate. Even the faculty, whose views may seem homogeneous if contrasted with those of the athletic director or the treasurer, will produce as many opinions as there are members on an admissions committee.

## Registrar and Admissions

In about one quarter of American colleges,[33] the vestigial connection between the admissions function and that of the registrar is retained by combining both in a single individual or placing one under the other. This organizational form is a kind of fossilized relic of the viewpoint that was dominant at the turn of the century and that grew out of faculty solicitude for minute specifications; it became important to record and keep track of the extent to which each student met or fell short of the specifications. When a high school principal wrote, "I recommend John Smith in algebra but not in French," the registrar's habits of thought were such that he could cope with the situation; the admissions officer could not, since John Smith was indivisible; someone had to say yes or no to his application as a person entire.

The viewpoint of the earlier faculty committees was of a piece with the entire "credits" approach to educational record keeping which has come to be characteristic of American higher education. The registrar is of necessity a central figure in this conception, so that to the extent that it pervades admissions practice, the registrar seemed the logical functionary to supervise admissions. The idea of small, interchangeable units of learning, redeemable at par, certified much as were the coins stamped by medieval goldsmiths, has been irresistibly practical and convenient, particularly in an educational environment characterized by a wide variety of colleges and universities. Yet in using this procedure most educators have felt somewhat uneasily that it partakes of the "fallacy of misplaced concreteness." The idea that measured fragments of experience can be deemed to persist and accumulate additively has a disquieting resemblance to the manner in which some chemical substances persist and accumulate in the human body, as for example in lead poisoning. Or, alternatively, if "dated" credits are used, the process resembles ingestion into the system of radioactive substances which decay at a rate depending on their half life—an even more disquieting parallel.

## Selection Problems

In recent years, faculty admissions committees in many colleges have assumed policy-making functions of a much broader scope, particularly in institutions which have become highly selective. These committees often raise far-reaching questions of general policy—questions so broad as to be unanswerable in any definitive sense because they involve profound philosophical issues about the aims of education, its functions in society, and the adaptability of various human types to versions of the educational process to which different colleges are committed. Sometimes special ad hoc committees have been set up to deal with these issues, and there is a considerable polemical literature in which individual faculty members wrestle with questions of educational policy.[34]

This more recent current of thought represents an almost complete reversal of the earlier emphasis in which admissions committees laid down detailed specifications about subjects of study. Two converging forces have brought about this reversal. One of these forces is the spread of the comprehensive high school, the general improvement of secondary education, and the consequent greatly improved articulation between secondary and higher education. A student having possible college attendance in mind is much more likely to be guided into a reasonably appropriate program and less likely to fall into one that is unacceptable to colleges than was the case a generation ago. Specific subject-matter requirements persist, but in diminishing degree, and they are more rational in the sense of fitting broad curricular objectives instead of reflecting arbitrary selections of "units" made at the whim of individual colleges.

The second force is the view of the more selective colleges that subject-matter requirements serve only as minimum qualifications. Nearly all candidates meet these requirements, so that the really difficult policy decisions involve selection from a group already "qualified." The grounds on which decision is based may seem arbitrary and capricious to one observer, while to another they may seem natural reflections of values deeply and sincerely held. In any case there are few guidelines, and the scope for disputation is vast. This is the area of "invisible" or "ambiguous" admissions requirements.[35] So it comes about that in selective colleges committees frequently find themselves trapped in prolonged sessions dealing with individual cases; relatively trivial differences among candidates turn the scales. Such decisions are basically ignorant decisions and may reflect whims and prejudices of individuals simply because no hard evidence is at hand. Schools complain of the difficulty of predicting admission decisions, and hence of advising students.[36]

A great deal of soul searching goes on about the kind of selection that should occur in these situations. Admissions officers look for "interesting," or "creative," or "original" candidates. They are, not unnaturally, drawn toward youngsters who have shown intellectual curiosity, exceptional energy or initiative, those who have pushed some unusual project to successful completion, or have demonstrated marked qualities of leadership. It is quite probable that many of these individuals will show exceptional achievement in the next 30 years, at least in the qualities and activities that our society values. But there are two defects in this kind of selection.

First, the criteria in all this selection are based on limited values and objectives. The college will gain through the splendor of its reputation as a place from which leaders come. But is this kind of gain good for the system as a whole? Perhaps these human focuses of imagination and energy would be more broadly effective and influential if scattered more widely among more diverse student bodies. Perhaps, in the wider view, the obligation to provide an education must, at some point, begin to outweigh the privilege of choosing whom one will seek out to educate. Nobody ever seems to question the usual Level Two approach, which simply assumes that this obligation does not exist, which pictures the college ranging the jungle, seeking whom it may devour, and richly entitled to whatever student material it can pounce upon, regardless of the effect on other colleges. Centers of excellence are, indeed, essential. But not if they are artificially constructed by depriving others; not if tighter selection is, in effect, made a substitute for education by assembling a group that will perform well under even the most dull and unimaginative tutelage. Excellence should be a product of the educational process and experience, not a product of exclusion that may do more harm than good.

The second defect is that all the factors that enter into "ambiguous" selection imply that we know a promising student when we see one. But our decisions are ignorant. Even if we set as a criterion merely the applicant's ability to shine in our existing academic environment, we miss the mark in many cases.[37] How much wider of the mark would we be if our students had access to the full range of nurture, stimulus, and excitement that a truly imaginative university environment would be capable of providing? As A. N. Whitehead said, only certain kinds of excellence are possible in particular historic epochs. It is entirely conceivable that some of the human types whom we reject as a matter of course would, under a different concept of life and its purpose, turn out to be most needed. No admissions officer can ever afford to forget the Ugly Duckling, Cinderella, or "the stone that the builders rejected."

The moral for admissions policy seems to be this: as a practical matter some floor has to be put under the level of preparation and apparent intellectual aptitude, in order to avoid tragic misfits. Even if the educational process is all wrong, we can't change it overnight. But above this floor, a good argument can be made for something like a random choice of applicants. Then each college will be more nearly carrying its fair share of the load of providing education. It will in time come to be judged by the "value added" to its alumni, and it will have the satisfaction of knowing that its achievement is inherent and earned, not adventitiously and artificially gained through shunting a super-select group into its gates.

In other words, we need to entertain the possibility that our society is not infallible in its characteristic judgments and values. Should our criteria for access to higher education turn out, in a longer perspective, to be limited and provincial, one way to mitigate their harmful impact would be by increasing the randomization of the selective process.

It is a basic principle of evolution, as well as of human affairs, that diversity is a chief source of progress.[38] Because we cannot begin to imagine all the kinds of diversity that might help us, we need to imitate nature by permitting random processes to play their unpredictable part. It has been well said that the universe is not only stranger than we imagine—it is stranger than we *can* imagine. The same is undoubtedly true of the depth and variety of ability concealed in human personality. The worst way to get at the truth is to start with the assumption that you have it already. For generations the universities of the old world have assumed that they knew how to select students. They tested their assumptions by pointing to the leaders the system produced. This argument had two fatal flaws: first, there was virtually no other source of leaders against which to measure the success of the system, and second, the real test of selection is the quality of the rejects. As the saying goes, the doctor can bury his mistakes. The university system has been able to render its mistakes invisible by condemning them to noneducation and hence, for the most part, to nonperformance—a perfect example of the self-fulfilling prophecy. We say to a candidate, or to a social group, "You are not able enough to benefit by education." We accordingly deprive him of education, he accomplishes little, and we can then point to the wisdom of our decision. Not only have American Negroes, a minority, been the victims of this reasoning. The European working classes as a group have been under the same disability for centuries, as have our working classes, too, to a smaller extent.[39]

The faculty admissions committee, then, started as a policy group, and in the beginning policy took the form of relatively minute subject-matter prescriptions. The evolution from this point has taken two main directions: some committees pay a great deal of attention to passing on individual cases, so much so that little time is left for thoughtful consideration of major policy questions. In other cases most individual decisions are left to an admissions staff, but the committee may devote a great deal of time to broad policy matters and the study of the long-range effects of alternative selection methods.

## Organization of Admissions

In *The Admissions Officer,* Jane Zech Hauser and Paul F. Lazarsfeld report on a comprehensive statistical survey, made in 1963 by the Bureau of Applied Social Research of Columbia University.[40] It is a survey of great utility because of its broad coverage of the admissions function in many colleges. The report tabulates questionnaire responses from 811 colleges, broadly representative, by type, of a universe of 1,299 colleges. A study of such breadth must of necessity confine itself largely to formal relationships and externals, and cannot penetrate deeply into the substance of admissions policy. Nevertheless this study contributes important evidence about the internal organization of the admissions function in colleges.

Eighty-seven percent of the respondents reported the existence of an admissions committee, but the functions of these committees are shown to vary widely. In some colleges the committee is purely advisory, in some it passes upon borderline cases, in others upon all. About 50 percent of the admissions officers responding were chairmen of their committees. According to the authors, "this can be taken as an indicator of influence." Many would dispute this conclusion. There are clear advantages in having a chairman chosen from the faculty, and in having the professional director use the committee as a maker of policy, as a sounding board, as a source of support, and as a generator of ideas. Particularly, in a working committee, the assignment of tasks by a chairman from the faculty who is not an administrative officer is likely to be accepted more willingly. The all-important goal of involving the faculty is promoted.

The sagacious admissions director maintains close relations with the faculty, both in and out of the committee. He keeps the faculty fully informed of admissions problems and admissions policy and involves them as much as possible in activities related to admissions. Colleges in which hostile faculty groups set out to investigate and alter admissions policy and procedure are likely to be those in which the faculty has not been kept informed, has no sense of participation, and in consequence often has quite erroneous ideas about the nature of admissions problems. A faculty that has been kept consistently informed, that has been consulted, that shares a sense of participation in admissions activities and an honest puzzlement at admissions dilemmas is not the kind of faculty in which "lynching parties" spontaneously form to attack the admissions office.

If an admissions officer jealously reserves to himself all activities and decisions regarding admissions he wholly misconceives the nature of his job. To be truly effective he must learn to work through many other people, and in this way greatly to multiply his efforts and effectiveness. He must work more by influence and persuasion than by authority. If he discovers a rebel in the faculty, he contrives to get him appointed chairman of a committee to grapple with the problem in all its complexity. A faculty deeply involved in the social and educational ramifications of the admissions process can contribute much to the making of a wise admissions policy. Furthermore, attention to the broad sociological aspects of admissions is an effective antidote for the minor pedantries to which even the most dedicated teachers are sometimes prone.

The admissions function should ramify not only through the faculty but also through all the activities of the institution that concern student personnel. Student counseling can be made more effective if information collected in connection with admissions is made fully available both to faculty advisers and to professional counselors.[41] It goes without saying that the confidentiality of this material must at all times be respected. Some admissions data may prove to be simply irrelevant to counseling needs. But in many admissions folders are concealed hints and suggestions of the dynamic and usually turbulent processes of change to which the late adolescent is exposed. He is in a stage in which his emotions outweigh his intellect, and his glands outvote his cortex. He is learning to establish his identity, to cut loose from emotional dependence on his parents, and, as the phrase goes, to discover who he is.[42]

He is seeking to understand and clarify his relations with the other sex; he is groping toward religious concepts which may be quite at variance with those in which he was brought up. And very often he is struggling to free himself from the presuppositions of the particular subculture in which he was nurtured, having for the first time come to realize that the environment of his childhood, with its attendant system of values, is not the whole world. All these adjustments carry the possibility of very great stress and turmoil. The admissions folder may contain hints of family situations which contribute to the student's current dilemma. The counselor cannot afford to be ignorant of this background material, even though the live student before him must remain the chief source of information.

It goes without saying that the administration of student financial aid, as grants, loans, or part-time jobs, must be closely coordinated with admissions. The two functions are increasingly coming to be administered under a single head.

Coordination with the college medical office is also essential. The procedures for securing health information before and after candidates' admission, particularly in the sensitive area of mental health, must be carefully worked out in cooperation with the medical director. Of particular importance is the maintenance of the professional confidentiality of medical records. The college physician should deal with the applicant's physician. The admissions officer may arrange matters but should serve in this area only as a lay recipient of advice.

The matter of coordination with the athletic department is such a sensitive and well-advertised topic that one is tempted simply to ignore it. It raises complicated issues beyond the scope of this discussion, yet it illustrates more perfectly than any other aspect of the admissions process the basic truth stated above that the way in which a college organizes itself internally to deal with admissions reflects its attitude about the meaning and purpose of the admissions function in the life of the institution. The area of sports provides the most extreme examples of collegiocentric, or Level Two, thinking. So essential are sports to the health and welfare of most young persons that it is easy to hide many abuses under the pretense that whatever concerns sports is good.

There is a place even for spectator sports, sedentary as they are, but it is questionable how far the colleges ought to exploit students to provide them. College administrations are usually so much under the spell of alumni thinking on this issue that they are well behind representative student thought. The type of alumnus who remains a perpetual sophomore is, however, coming to be less common than the student of a new generation who has a realistic view of what he wants from education.

Whatever compromise a given college makes between the admissions and the athletic interest, it is above all important that the relationship be known and clearly defined. The less the admissions process is distorted and corrupted by the concept of spectator sports as a concomitant of higher education, the better the odds that a sane policy of truly amateur sport with wide participation, and with genuine excitement, will come into being.

Cooperation by alumni can be an important and legitimate asset in the admissions process, yet in the past generation or two, there have been glaring abuses in this area. The key to wise utilization of alumni lies in the conviction that the central purpose of alumni participation should be educational guidance, with a subsidiary yet sometimes useful aim of aiding the process of selection. A mature graduate of any college or university should be able to convey to a high school student some conception of the values inherent in higher education in general, and also some notion of what goes on in his own alma mater, including its prevailing customs, attitudes, and beliefs. Discussion with such a person can be a valuable experience for the youngster groping toward a definition of his interests and confronted also by the practical necessity of deciding what college to aim at. Though there are exceptions, effective communication with teenagers is usually easier for younger than for older alumni. Younger alumni are also more likely to know the college as it is today and are less likely than their older confreres to be under the spell of ancient and outmoded educational ideas.

In point of fact, alumni recruiting usually has been the focus of peculiarly virulent Level Two, collegiocentric, thinking. Not all inter-college competition is bad; the danger lies in the sort of ignorant decisions to which all college recruiters are prone. Recruiting implies that one knows a good candidate when one sees him. The judgments involved in this process are heavily loaded with personal and class predilections, prejudices, and assumptions, all held with such conviction that they seem, to the holder, to be self-evident truths or laws of nature. So we see the enthusiastic alumnus, aflame with competitive fervor, exerting all his persuasive arts to steer toward his own college particular students who satisfy his image of how the ideal alumnus-in-the-making should look. Undoubtedly some of these attractive youngsters will turn out extremely well. But with the eye of long experience one easily imagines all those others, whose promise, at this stage well concealed, will eventually be greater, who somehow do not get picked up in this process, so uncomfortably reminiscent of fraternity rushing.

Yet carefully chosen alumni, painstakingly briefed in the essential values of the situation, can provide most helpful guidance. This is particularly true if they maintain communication with local high schools. The school will know quickly enough how to distinguish the high-powered "recruiters" from those willing to align their efforts with the school's own low pressure, long-range objectives of sound educational guidance. One good way of judging and comparing the true educational merit of the admissions policies of various colleges is to talk to the high school guidance counselors in the high schools. Their objectives are basically educational, their stance toward the world of intercollege competition is neutral, and they have a basic identification with the student himself and his interests.

The alumnus must realize that he is not an "agent" of the college in the sense of being authorized to make commitments on admissions or financial aid. He must be prepared to see a young favorite of his, with whose interests he has identified himself, refused in the general selection process, perhaps in favor of some other competitor in a distant city; and he must be prepared for occasions when his verdict for or against a candidate will be overruled by a preponderance of other evidence. His firsthand impression, based on brief acquaintance, is a valid and useful contribution, but the school, which has watched the student perform for three or four years, may have more convincing and contradictory evidence. Above all he needs to be restrained from his loyal impulse to compete first and think afterwards.

Finally, no admissions operation is completely developed unless it maintains some effective cooperation with student government and student thinking. In one sense, college undergraduates can offer the best educational guidance of all, because from them prospective students can get the true "low-down" on the college, untainted by catalog rhetoric or official pretense. Their enthusiasm, if it exists, is contagious and genuine, their strictures realistic. Such functions as campus hospitality and the guiding of visitors are peculiarly appropriate as student activities. Perhaps most effective of all is the informal relationship of the student with his own high school, usually unorganized and unorganizable. Some communication with student government or with student committees that evince an interest is evidence that the admissions office is alert to student opinion and prepared to consult and cooperate with student groups. It is one more small contribution to preventing student alienation from the purposes of the institution.

The foregoing discussion shows at once how vital the intelligent administration of admissions can be to the educational welfare of a college, and how little it depends on the formal exercise of authority by the admissions officer. His task is in the broadest sense an educational one of bringing his colleagues in the faculty and administration into constant and repeated contact with the problems and dilemmas of admissions and involving them in admissions and guidance activities. His task and that of his staff is one of influence, persuasion, organization; it is to create an atmosphere in which his associates gain a deeper appreciation of the sociology of higher education, and its roots in the society around it, especially in the secondary schools. College teachers can be counted on to recognize cases in which the wrong applicant has been admitted; they need to learn to worry even more about cases in which the wrong applicant was rejected or, what is worse, discouraged from applying. Admissions is one of the main tap roots connecting an institution to the society that sustains and judges it.

# 4. College Admissions as a System

## The System Concept

The movement of students through the elementary and secondary school systems, their redistribution among many phases of higher education, and the forces and motives that cause them to persist or drop out, all constitute a vast social process. This is a system in the classic sense of a whole with interrelated parts—an organism rather than a mechanism. Everyone is aware of this interrelationship, yet in the actual procedures and motivations connected with the entry of students into colleges it is usually ignored because the interests of individual students and individual colleges are the dominant forces. Only recently have we begun to compile statistics that are comprehensive enough to make it possible to study the system as a whole, or to begin to make a judgment of how far the uncoordinated self-regarding action of a multiplicity of individual institutions does in fact contribute to the overall public welfare. We have too easily assumed that the public interest is served by turning everyone loose in a competitive scramble.

The result is that little thought or discussion is directed to Level Three, which may be roughly defined as "admissions and the public interest," or, more broadly, "admissions as a system." Yet this is a topic of increasing relevance. The focusing of Congressional attention upon higher education and the channeling of federal funds in the same direction will raise insistent questions about quality differentials, because in their "system" behavior, our many institutions, taken together, constitute a great, interacting complex. An increasing literature about new, developing countries puts education at the center of the forces that make for economic and cultural growth. The nature of these problems, both in the United States and abroad, enforces a systems viewpoint both upon the government operations that seek to further educational development and upon the studies by social scientists that seek to appraise and measure this development. This viewpoint has, however, been slower in appearing in the United States, which is older (in a certain sense), much bigger, and less self-consciously "developing."

There is in the United States, it is true, a good deal of intercollege activity devoted to joint action of narrowly specific kinds. Regional pacts for cooperation among colleges and universities are one example. The formation of the College Entrance Examination Board in 1900, for the specific purpose of standardizing admissions requirements and providing tests, was an earlier case in point.[43] The more recent work of the College Scholarship Service in organizing the evaluation of student financial need also filled a lack that all the colleges felt. Though a vast amount of discussion has gone into the organization and conduct of services such as these, little of it has included the Level Three point of view. These organizations and the areas of discussion that envelop them have a Level Two bias. Large groups of colleges have been able, in the pursuit of their own individual ends, to agree on these measures only because the measures are designed to run parallel to the interests of each, and so are to a large extent noncontroversial. Cooperative agencies among colleges tend to include activities in which the interests of the members run parallel. The really difficult problems at Level Three concern differential interests among colleges, the areas of conflict and competition in which the ostensible or supposed interest of the college runs counter to the public interest, or to that of individual students, or to that of other colleges. Such conflicts form a natural and inevitable aspect of the ecology of higher education. It is significant that little progress has been made in joint admissions procedures, clearing systems, timing control, and the like, or in control of the "raiding" of faculties, because these measures touch the sensitive areas of competitive recruiting. These relationships resemble the interaction, sometimes hostile, sometimes cooperative and symbiotic, among living species. The relationships between competing species, or between predator and prey, though involving sharp conflicts of individual interest, contribute to the balance of nature.

It is something of an historical accident as mentioned above that a major "switching point" in education should occur at the end of the twelfth grade. Any division of the educational process into periods is in part arbitrary, as is illustrated by the long, inconclusive controversy about the usefulness of the junior high school. That controversy itself is merely a special case of the more general problem of subdividing the 12-year sequence. Though this segmentation is arbitrary, it exists and will not quickly be done away with. Custom and habit as well as vested interests in particular administrative arrangements are strong forces tending to perpetuate the status quo.

As pointed out earlier, the decisions that determine the sorting among colleges are guided by a certain substratum of factual knowledge about higher education, supplemented by a vast, amorphous, and confused body of beliefs, rumors, folklore, and gossip. This situation is true both of students in choosing colleges and of colleges in choosing students. Although the criteria of choice have intellectual and academic dimensions, they lie predominantly in the field of cultural anthropology and sociology.[44]

A generation or two ago the fact that only a small fraction of students "went on" to college made the conclusion of high school a natural breaking point. Now, though we are entering an era in which a substantial majority of all high school graduates continue their formal education, the custom of a general redistribution at this stage, once established, is reinforced by the momentum of long habit, by the complex variety and differentiation of colleges, and by the fact that the four-year undergraduate college is the only stage in the educational process that imposes heavy financial cost on the student. Free education through the secondary level is generally available to all, while at the postgraduate university level a variety of financial aids, now greatly augmented by government funds, facilitates the progress of qualified students. There is much taking of thought, exploration, soul-searching, and "shopping around" as the grade 12 switching point approaches, for it leads students directly into a four-year period that is expensive for almost all of them and indispensable for an increasing proportion of them.

The diversity that exists among American colleges and universities has given rise to an extensive literature. A whole school of sociology has arisen out of efforts to study and differentiate the relative "climates" of different colleges. Ways of "fitting" the student to the college have become prominent topics in current discussions. This work is admirable and ingenious and needs to be pressed further. But in these "typologies" there is little that is normative. The student is encouraged to look for an environment that in some sense "fits" him. There is nothing wrong with this attitude, but perhaps the same amount of thought devoted to the more general problem of how one goes about getting an education (with such help as one can find in a college—any college) would be more rewarding. The question also arises whether "consumers' research" publicizing these differences may tend to sharpen them, perhaps reducing the encounter of differing human types and views that is of the essence of education.

The exuberant variety of colleges and universities in the United States is an asset of incalculable value. Free enterprise and initiative function in parallel with state-operated education to produce the world's most diverse, as well as the world's most chaotic, educational system. It may prove also to be the world's most vigorous and effective, but it poses special problems for the student, functioning as he does at Level One.

In particular, the legacy of the English university colleges has exerted a curious effect on our system. In this tradition the student is not merely affiliated with the college (which is of course residential) ; he is enveloped and engulfed in it. The college is responsible for his entire formation, not only intellectual but social, moral, and physical. This situation is in sharp contrast to the more casual and shifting connection of students with universities in the European continental tradition. So close an envelopment generates powerful, lifelong loyalties. The American phenomenon of alumni loyalty to an undergraduate college is in large measure traceable to the English tradition.

Much that is valuable has come from this tradition, but it has had one unfortunate effect. The student's system of values gives a central position to the objective of getting into "the college of his choice." Once this vantage point is gained, he is tempted to relax and think of education as something beneficial that will be done to him, not something he gets for himself. This is the almost inevitable result of the undue stress put upon affiliation with the "right" college. The Pierian draught must come from the proper jug with the proper label, or it has no magic. The obvious convenience of this tradition to stimulate alumni financial support has been in one sense a boon to education, while at the same time it has furthered an irrational particularism that distracts attention from the main issue, that is, the educational process itself. The American student thinks of himself as wedded for life to his college, a view the college is delighted to encourage. There is little of the movement from one university to another that for generations exerted a civilizing effect on European students.

It may well be that in the large urban universities that have a tradition opposite to that of close nurture in a fostering environment, other values will emerge. The shifting clientele of these institutions, less distracted by particularistic institutional loyalties, driving fiercely toward the heart of the educational process itself, may recover some of the medieval flavor of the university as the product of student initiative.

The conventional discussion of college admissions, pitched as it is at Level Two, is based on selection of students.[45] In the era now coming upon us, in which perhaps three-fourths of all high school graduates will be going on to some kind of higher education, selection becomes an inappropriate method of sorting. For if selection is to have social utility, there must be a large, undifferentiated group of rejects whom one can dismiss from consideration, because they are taken care of in other ways. The system is not designed or expected to take account of them. Under the conditions now approaching, the primitive device of application-and-reply becomes unbearably clumsy and inappropriate unless heavily supplemented by other expedients. The problem becomes one of guidance, often of redirection, to bring about a gradual regrouping and classification of students, looking toward the movements of groups with differing talents and interests into various appropriate categories of further education.

The forces that lead a given student to apply to a specific college constitute, in the aggregate, a more far-reaching and effective sorting device than the small amount of selectivity the college is able to exercise among the relatively few students who have gone so far as to seek it out and fill out applications for it. In other words, preselection by the student and by his advisers is a more pervasive and powerful force for sorting than is selection by colleges. The heavy investment of most colleges in recruitment of students, and in public relations directed toward this end, is a tacit admission of the importance of preselection.

Insofar as selection by the college itself is effective, it is mainly a process exerted at second hand. The student, and in particular those who guide him, tend to anticipate shrewdly the action of the college. Admissions committees "telegraph their punches." Applicants avoid colleges they believe are likely to refuse them and concentrate on those more likely to accept them. So the "system" view of admissions discloses a network of probabilities continuously in process of weighing, revision, and correction, with alert guidance officers serving to mediate the forces of supply and demand.

## Abandoned Clienteles

In the past generation or two there has existed on a wholesale scale a process by which colleges "run away" from their natural clienteles. What defines the natural clientele of a college? Basically the geographic determinant is the most powerful.[46] The natural clientele is made up predominantly of local or nearby students and is commonly limited to a particular segment or stratum of these. For denominational colleges, the natural clientele is the denomination. Beyond these, there are socioeconomic determinants leading to the selection of high- or low-cost institutions, and there are ethnic groups and subcultures prone to seek particular kinds of education. Programs that have a professional or vocational slant have long had a special appeal for socially mobile, upward-striving youngsters, particularly those of immigrant background seeking a firmer place and improved status in an inhospitable culture.

Insofar as a college serves its natural clientele, it is adhering to its basic obligation to provide education to those needing it. A college "runs away" from its natural clientele when it replaces this clientele with other groups, though this may be done for what it regards as cogent reasons. A conspicuous trend of this kind has involved the now highly selective colleges that served mainly local clienteles a generation or two ago. The rapid growth of the demand for education enabled them to "raise their standards" and attract on a nationwide scale applicants thought to be especially well qualified. This effort was reinforced by financial aid deliberately planned to encourage geographical diversification. There are genuine educational values in such diversification, and the colleges quote distinguished authorities from George Washington down in support of it. So it is that many of these colleges have come to serve a national clientele, leaving a much larger stratum of less prestigious and commonly newer institutions to meet the needs of the preponderant group who must go to school near home. The new clientele, more diverse in geographical origin, typically grows more homogeneous in its preponderance of students from high-income families of the managerial and professional classes.

For the selective college, this has been a matter of self-congratulation because of "higher standards." Looked at from the obverse, it is rather a matter of abandoning one clientele and replacing it with another. Higher standards of student selection have not inevitably led to higher standards of teaching. In some cases the opposite is true: colleges have brought in students so able that they may succeed in wringing an education out of quite outmoded and uninspired teaching; but not always. Boredom on the part of bright freshmen in courses attuned to the freshmen of yesteryear has pointed up situations in which student quality has outrun teaching quality. College faculties that a generation ago had been complaining about "poor preparation" shifted smoothly and imperceptibly into complaints about "student apathy." Though there has been a gain in regional diversity, it has been offset by a reduction in the diversity of socioeconomic origins.

How far the abandonment of a clientele is justifiable depends, among other things, on how adequately the abandoned clientele can be taken care of in other ways. Assuming that they are adequately accommodated by a shift into nearby colleges, there still remains the question of how far it is educationally desirable and in the public interest to concentrate the ablest students in a few institutions. Up to a certain point this concentration is undoubtedly useful and stimulating. "Centers of excellence" are not wholly mythical. But the arguments are not all on one side, and it is entirely possible that in the end more would be accomplished by having more high ability spread more widely as a stimulating influence. The argument is in part academic because nature takes good care that first-rate ability keeps turning up in the unlikeliest places. So no small group of colleges, however prestigious, is likely to corner the market for high ability.

It is probably true that for many colleges that have become much more selective in recent years, "higher standards" represent a student group that is intellectually somewhat abler. Whether this change has been accompanied by a concurrent improvement in the educational process is quite another and more dubious question. The pressure of applications has often made for fatuous complacency among college faculties who reason that if what they have to offer is so sought after, it must be very good. The non sequitur in this reasoning rarely comes to light because of the ardor and energy of students sufficiently determined to extract an education for themselves even from uninspired offerings.

Another conspicuous example of abandoning a clientele is found in the history of many denominational colleges. These colleges were founded, typically, to hold young people in the fold—to meet the need for education but to supply one purged of secular and worldly influences. Too many faculties strong in piety were less impressive in learning and intellectual stature. The demand for higher intellectual standards ran counter to the ideal of doctrinal purity. The need for cash customers often made it desirable to accept students outside the fold, and their presence intensified the demand for an education more broadly based. The denominational clientele were thus often largely unprovided for, except as they were willing to accept an education quite different from what the founders had envisaged.[47] The early twentieth century accordingly witnessed a wholesale shift from denominational to nonsectarian control.

Something of the same flight from an established clientele may be occurring in the hitherto predominantly Negro colleges. The stronger ones reach toward a national clientele, while the beginnings of integration reduce the number of places that might earlier have gone to nearby Negro students badly in need of education at low cost. All these shifts in clientele tend to be thought of, by the individual colleges concerned, as gains and improvements; actually they may or may not be. What is certain is that they represent departure from earlier objectives and shifts in the direction of institutional purpose.

## Ignorant Selection

It is not strange that the "systems" view of college admissions has been neglected. Students, like other consumers, are unorganized. In the typical case, the choice of a college, like the choice of a mate, is a once-in-a-lifetime problem; the individual copes with it as best he can and moves on. There is little incentive to gain practice and experience in the art of shopping for an education. Colleges are invincibly atomistic. Not only do independent institutions pursue their own supposed interests undeviatingly, often at the expense of the student's long-range interest; even the several local constituent units of a single state system, all under the same control, eye each other jealously and compete intensely in recruiting. Some of this may redound to the student's benefit, but much of it simply ignores the effect a student's choice of college may have on him. It is not permissible to suggest that one's own institution should not be, if all the facts were truly evaluated, the very best bargain for nearly every one.

Each college strenuously seeks the "best" students. To the extent that marks and tests come to take the central position as means of evaluation, this imposes a unidimensional scale by which to value human talent. The scale, it is true, stresses a set of verbal and quantitative capabilities, and a knack for dealing with abstractions that are of central importance in a wide range of human affairs, especially the intellectual disciplines. But it tends to enforce a one-sided and narrow view of the full range of human talent. It conceals the depth of our ignorance about the dynamics of human personality and about the rich diversity of ways in which human ability manifests itself.

The highly selective colleges, faced with a superfluity of candidates "qualified" by conventional criteria, find themselves falling back increasingly on subjective appraisals. These lead to ignorant decisions based on hunches or upon unconscious predispositions about personality types. There is, indeed, serious question whether, above a certain "floor" of ability, the college and the public would not be better served by random selection of candidates than by the kind of ignorant purposefulness many admissions committees delight to exercise.

David Riesman, echoing A. N. Whitehead's thought already cited, says "I believe that only certain ideas will be generated and catch on under any given socioeconomic conditions." The accustomed and largely unconscious scheme of values that characterizes our culture must, like all others, have its blind spots. The evaluations that we intuitively regard as least disputable may, in fact, be the very ones that conceal these blind spots. As Irving Lorge has pointed out, it is only the imperfections of our selective processes that make them tolerable. This is only another way of saying that a healthy degree of randomization has sneaked in through the back door. Our earnest but ignorant purposefulness undoubtedly excludes some variants, some types of excellence which we are not capable of recognizing or even of imagining. So it is reasonable to suggest that intense selectivity, beyond some point or other, brings diminishing returns. There is more to gain by improving the entire educational process across the board, than by segregating for education in particular environments either the few who are so able that they can develop in almost any environment, or a group homogeneous in the sense that it corresponds to our blundering and ignorant notions of excellence.

## Value—and "Value Added"

Colleges love to "point with pride" to the achievements of their alumni. The achievements are real enough, but they are often due not so much to the educational processes of the college as to the forces that have concentrated in that college, people with particular interests and abilities. The college, in other words, serves less as an educational influence than as a traffic interchange—a switching and concentrating force to bring together for four years people likely in any case to proceed to certain educational and occupational goals. Thus A. W. Astin has shown that much of the apparent high "productivity" of certain colleges in turning out PH.D.s in science is traceable to their attraction for students already strongly conditioned by inclination and ability to proceed in this direction.[48] The attraction exerted by these colleges is of course not at all the same thing as the selectivity they may exercise among their applicants for admission. The work of A. W. Astin, John L. Holland, and D. L. Thistlethwaite using National Merit Scholarship Corporation data is an important contribution to the study of access to education on a "systems" basis, and an antidote to exaggerated claims for the differential effectiveness of particular colleges.

What we need to measure, if measurement is to be resorted to at all, is something akin to the "value added by manufacture" as this term is used by the U.S. Bureau of the Census. The "value added" by four years in a particular college may in individual cases be large, but more often it is only moderate, and the social effectiveness of graduates is traceable in great measure to the antecedent quality of the entering students. Nor can this be regarded necessarily as an argument for high selectivity, since so much of the effect is traceable to the preselection on the part of the student and his advisers, which must first occur before he is brought within the ambit of the college's selective process.

## Models of Student Distribution

To represent the "system" behavior of the entire college admission process, one can distinguish a number of oversimplified models, each an extreme case of how such a system might operate. Granted that what actually happens is a mixture of all these, such caricatures help to clarify the problem by sorting out the kinds of forces that seem to be operating. Some of the more obvious models would be the following.

Since in this country 80 percent of college students attend colleges within their state of residence, it is probably safe to conclude that geographic propinquity is the strongest single force leading to choice of a college. Though the strongest, it is by no means the only force, because, depending on the populousness of a state, and the complexity of its educational system, much scope remains for the exercise of other forces as well. State boundaries are of course arbitrary. In a large and populous state that has a wide variety of colleges, students can stay near home and still find wide opportunity to follow educational preferences based on reasons other than propinquity. In other states the range of opportunity may be restricted to a handful of institutions of limited variety in type or quality. Though here the incentive to go farther afield is greater, to do so is expensive, so that many will find themselves in colleges less well adapted to their needs and preferences. The recent marked tendency of state institutions to discriminate against out-of-state applicants, as places become scarcer, is increasing the validity of this model and increasing the provinciality of the education offered by each of the 50 states.

Because of the arbitrariness of state boundaries, some of the "cuckoo states" have depended unduly on nearby institutions across state borders for the educational nourishment of their youth. To the extent that this has occurred, even the 20 percent of students who attend college outside their own states are moved in large measure by the basic force of propinquity. This is a phenomenon that has characterized several populous eastern states in which an old educational tradition of private colleges and universities long inhibited adequate development of publicly supported education.

Logically next on the list of models, but numerically much less important, is the opposite kind of situation, in which students seek out the most distant opportunities in order to maximize the benefits of geographical diversification. This tendency, pressed to its utmost, brings an increase in interregional and international study, with all the educational benefits of intercultural experience. Such cosmopolitan exposure, despite its undisputed value, can affect only a small minority of students. In terms of numbers of students involved, it represents a far weaker force for college selection than does propinquity.

Quite different in principle is a model in which the strongest institutions attract the ablest students. This concept is simplistic in that it leaves unanswered a tangle of questions about which are the strongest institutions and which the ablest students. In complex universities different undergraduate schools may properly have widely differing "standards," and it is in any case an oversimplified abstraction to measure the varieties of effective human talent on a single, unidimensional scale. There may be, too, some divergence between true excellence in a college and the sort of prestigious reputation that can attract applicants. One must allow for the inevitable human tendency to want what others seem to be running after; fads and fashions come to play a part. Yet despite such limitations, objective support for this model can be found. A. W. Astin and John L. Holland have shown that there is a strong tendency for "high-endowment" private institutions to attract abler students than "low-endowment" private institutions, and a somewhat less pronounced tendency for "high-budget" public institutions to attract abler students than "low-budget" institutions.[49]

The basic rationale of this model, from the standpoint of the public interest, resembles that of free, competitive enterprise in the economic world. Insofar as a college succeeds legitimately in meeting the needs of its clientele, there is a certain presumption that it is promoting the public welfare by following its own institutional self-interest. In Adam Smith's classic phrase, the businessman attending industriously and selfishly to his own affairs "is led by an invisible hand to promote an end which is no part of his intention"—that is, the general welfare. Hence his view that a man is "never so harmlessly employed as when making money." The congeniality of this concept to the characteristic American ethos of independent individual initiative was bound to produce an educational system that looks chaotic in contrast to the hierarchical European universities, designed by and for an old and stratified culture.

Serious imperfections and counterforces exist to mar the perfection of this model, both in the world of commerce and the world of education. For example, many of the strongest institutions are also the most expensive. Though they are able to extend much financial aid to students who have "demonstrated need," this need is defined in relation to high and rapidly rising educational costs, so that even the "needy" student may come from a relatively well-to-do family. The student body as a whole, since it represents upper socioeconomic strata, may include a good many who lack the ferocity of all-out effort typical of the hard-up youngster who has only himself to depend on. Students may be sought for purposes thought to benefit the institution rather than the student, on the reasoning that the ultimate purpose of the institution is to benefit students, and that this end justifies a wide variety of means. Such reasoning may become farfetched and tenuous if used to fill up a weak department, or to supply teams for spectator sports. So it is not always safe to say that a college is never so harmlessly employed as when recruiting students.

The fourth model is one in which students distribute themselves into categories separated by clearly defined educational and vocational objectives. This is a model of commanding significance. Between 20 and 25 percent of undergraduate degrees in the United States go to students preparing for teaching below the college level. About 16 percent are in business administration, 10 percent in engineering, 6 percent in fine arts, 3 percent in agriculture, and 3 percent in home economics. These six fields account for more than 60 percent.[50] The remaining 40 percent might be thought of as "liberal arts" students and hence nonvocational; yet in fact vocational objectives are likely to be concealed in many majors in the so-called liberal arts colleges, particularly in natural sciences, social sciences, mathematics, and languages. It is only with the help of these concealed vocational objectives that many small liberal arts colleges manage to compete with the larger and better-financed state institutions many of which have curriculums that are overtly and unashamedly vocational. Public institutions are freer from the kind of inhibitions that caused the economics department of one leading women's college to be dissuaded from offering a course in accounting because this would be a "useful" subject.

The model that implies a basically vocational motivation reflects the widespread habit of looking on education as a means, not an end. It reflects the motives of the upward striving youth, seeking to better himself, willing to "hire himself educated," and uncritical of the means for accomplishing this. He may be limited in the breadth of his horizons, not necessarily interested in "ideas," but driving with intense energy toward a degree as a key to professional advancement. It is to be expected that a society in the midst of a vast expansion of higher education will place a high value on such considerations. In such a society, many youngsters will not have attained the degree of intellectual sophistication of the "academic" student, who can regard education as an open-ended process, potentially leading toward any one of a number of unforeseen destinations. The latter is able to contemplate changes in direction as he proceeds with the exploration he properly regards as the very essence of education. Between these extremes lies a complete spectrum of human types and of concepts of education. The model represents a central mode in our current mores. It is also convenient for purposes of analyses, in that it can be tied to definite, objectively determined categories and can be adjusted in a satisfying way to statistics of manpower needs in the economy.

A fifth model that can be conceived is one in which the "atmosphere" of a college plays a large part in determining the student's choice. Traditionally, information about the social, intellectual, and psychological climate of various colleges has been spread in covert, informal, and unorganized ways, by hearsay, rumor, and personal report. Only in the last few years has the college as a study in social psychology become a popular field of research. Behavioral scientists more recently have sought to define the "press," the loose congeries of impressions and pressures that constitute the student's environment in a college. To treat the college itself as a field of sociological and anthropological study has been a novel idea, somewhat frightening to both administrators and members of the more traditional disciplines. As Nevitt Sanford has pointed out, the reaction of college faculties has been defensive. They have felt threatened by this intrusion into an area in which a certain mystique had come to prevail. It was one thing to live in an accustomed climate where doctrinal disputes, though frequent and vehement, were comfortably inconclusive. It was quite another to be the subject of cold-eyed, dispassionate investigation marshaling objective evidence.

One could devote a volume to comparison of the many typologies of colleges and of college students that have emerged from these studies, which are of great interest educationally and sociologically. For the present purpose, it is enough to say that the studies are important because they help to trace what kinds of students tend to go to what kinds of colleges. This effort is plagued by a kind of concealed circularity in reasoning, which is difficult to get rid of for the reason that its extent is hard to measure. One can, of course, categorize colleges by quite arbitrary and conventional descriptions such as "public colleges," or "Catholic colleges," or "nonsectarian liberal arts colleges," or by such variables as size, cost, selectivity, and the like. Such descriptions do not go very deep.

In the effort to go deeper, a number of investigators have worked out categories based on the psychological "press" of institutions, using questionnaires to students to search out student attitudes, backgrounds, values, tastes, habits, and beliefs. This is a reasonsable procedure, since it is clear that an important, if not the chief, determinant of the press upon the individual is the kind of student who populates the college. The chief influence on students, in other words, is exerted by or mediated through their peer groups. These generate and apply most of the "press." But then, having categorized colleges, the researcher goes on to ask what kinds of students go to each college. He finds himself undertaking this investigation by asking another sample of students (typically high school graduates about to enter college) much the same kinds of questions already asked college students in the effort to categorize colleges. The net upshot of the operation is the conclusion that on the whole the kinds of students (as determined by questionnaires) that go to a particular college resemble the kinds of students that already attend the college (as determined by another set of questionnaires). Although this is of course an oversimplification of the situation, it still seems clear that an element of circularity must creep into investigations of this sort.

A. W. Astin, in his study, *Who Goes Where to College?*[51] seeks to get outside the circle, at least in part, by tying his categorization of students to broad occupational goals and accepting the not unreasonable assumption that "a person's choice of a vocation depends to some extent on his abilities, values, goals, attitudes, and other personal traits." He accepts uncritically John L. Holland's proposal that there are six groups of occupations corresponding to six basic personality types: realistic, scientific (or intellectual), social, conventional, enterprising, and artistic. This is a thoughtful and ingenious classification, and so great are the difficulties of any such classification process that it would be rash to assert a priori that a better one could be developed. Yet any such categorization obviously depends on so many arbitrary and peremptory decisions about the human types needed for or prevalent in specific occupations that it must raise serious doubts about results that depend on them.

Such efforts to relate student types to types of colleges raise, however, a broader range of issues, which would still be present even if the methodologies were unexceptionable. One possible use of such material is to try to fit students into the particular environments they will find congenial or stimulating, or adapted to their needs, or calculated to serve their purposes. This effort would accord with the proposals of David Riesman and others that some kind of "consumers' report" be available for different colleges so that the prospective student can know in advance what he is buying. To the extent that such a device prevents the student from getting into a college he is not up to (an unlikely contingency) or from getting into a college not up to him (which is much more probable), it could be useful. One wonders whether the net result might be an intensification of "typing," so that the student seeking a college looks for a student environment that most nearly fits his own subculture, origins, values, and attitudes. Any such tendency would reduce the variety of the social "mix" that is an indispensable ingredient in all education. The invincible propensity of most human beings to associate with others as nearly like themselves as possible is a contra-educational force of great power. It is only partly offset by the innate adventurousness of a minority who are stimulated by people different from themselves. Only the more intrepid succeed in overcoming this pull toward security, which represents the basic need for roots, stability, and an environment that is comprehensible and predictable.

There are long-range forces at work that may reduce the need and the significance of "typing," or of fitting the student to the college environment. Despite the persuasive advantages of the small college environment when functioning at its best, the long-term competitive forces appear to favor the larger institution. It can offer to the student a range of choice, and to the faculty a professional opportunity, and both of them a degree of stimulation and variety hard to equal in any small environment, particularly if it is isolated. By imaginative expedients of organization, large student bodies can be subdivided in ways that offset the student's feeling of faceless anonymity. Student disturbances are a sign that we have not yet seriously grappled with these problems, not a proof that the problems are insoluble. To the extent that student groups can be so organized, the large university unit has the great advantage that it can accommodate within itself many subcultures, and shifting "congenial minorities," which still need not be isolated. These stimulate each other, are open to interchange, and may work to offset the kind of ingrown patterning that so often characterizes isolated small colleges.

## Optimum Distribution

These then are some of the forces at work in effecting "the great sorting" of students among colleges. The sorting occurs among a rapidly evolving and changing set of institutions. Two major questions arise in studying it. The first question that pioneer studies like those of C. R. Pace, John L. Holland, A. W. Astin seek to answer is, essentially, "What is happening?" The objective is description and analysis. At least a start has been made toward answering this question. But if the ultimate object is to study not merely college admissions as a system, but "college admissions and the public interest," there is the much more difficult problem of trying to decide what the sorting *ought* to be. This normative purpose has been little thought about, beyond repeating the ideal prescription that each student ought to have as much education as he can digest and use.

We shall have to begin to clarify ideas beyond this stage. For example, given the present assortment of 2,000 colleges, universities, and junior colleges, what is the optimum way of distributing students among them, taking the long-run public interest as the criterion? Does the present scheme of things, representing an intricate mix of all the models sketched above, approximate the ideal of the classical assumptions about free enterprise? Would it be better, for example, to change the structure of the institutions by encouraging them to merge or to subdivide, than to try to change the distribution of students? One way to relieve the undue pressure on older, prestigious universities is to establish new ones intended, of set purpose, to surpass the old in quality. The new British universities, such as Sussex, or the new Santa Cruz campus of the University of California represent imaginative efforts in this direction.

The need for innovation and experiment to strengthen the educational process everywhere, and to increase its vitality is overwhelmingly great. If competitive recruiting can be a means to this end, let us by all means have it. What we seem to lack now, and what gives rise to doubts about competitive recruiting, is evidence of a direct coupling between advances in educational quality and recruiting appeal. The student himself, to say nothing of his parents and advisers, scarcely realizes the extent to which his real need is not just to learn but to acquire the habit and technique of learning and the appetite to go on with it indefinitely. In the public consciousness, education associates itself still, to a large extent, with the concept of a fixed corpus of knowledge that must be mastered, and the further concept of this mastering as instrumental—as the key to prescribed preferment and lifetime competency. A degree or a certificate is something negotiable and tangible to wave at a potential employer.

It would be unrealistic to hope for neat or definitive answers to large questions of this kind. Higher education in the United States is too complex and vast to lend itself to more than a modicum of central, purposeful control. Though mutual emulation tends toward some degree of uniformity, and governmental policy can exert salutary influence in some general directions, there is, in a certain large sense, nobody "in charge." Even governmental policies, weighted with the power of financial resources, constitute only one of many forces acting. Many aspects of change, of amelioration, must remain in the hands of the thousands of individuals whose decisions, decentralized and seemingly unrelated, will collectively determine the ponderous movements of the national rudder.

It is for this reason that educators collectively, though primarily concerned with their local decisions, need the habit of looking at the system as a whole. An infusion of thinking at Level Three in the training and the habitual practice of all concerned with college admissions can do much to broaden their perspective. A step forward for many of these people would be the mere realization that such a concept as Level Three exists and its criteria are different from those to which they are accustomed. This realization could influence their day-to-day task as they grope, according to their lights, toward the fulfillment of their annual quotas of students.

The study of college admissions as a system will inevitably merge, as time goes on, into the broader study of higher education in its totality as a system. A decade ago we were startled by the high proportion of able high school students who failed to continue their education. This proportion is decreasing rapidly, partly through increased financial aid, partly through a heightened public consciousness of the importance of education. In one respect our concept of higher education remains primitive. We speak of "going on to college," a simple idea, inherited from nineteenth-century practice. But just over the horizon we can sense two important changes in this oversimplified view.

As the first of these changes we shall see important new departures in the teaching and learning process at the undergraduate level. Undoubtedly more will be learned faster, but more important, what is learned will have increased relevance to the process of lifelong education, to cultivating the habit of learning and the appetite for it. For the first time, we shall educate for coping with a changing environment. College faculties will be relieved of much of the expository labor of education so that they may devote more time to their unique and indispensable function of interacting with students—needling, stimulating, questioning, browbeating, and encouraging. This interchange, which is the essence of education, can be greatly strengthened if the student has full and convenient recourse to film, television, records, tape, and similar aids to exposition. These will free the teacher's time for more important and personal interaction and will bring the student to a higher level of preparation to take his part in this dialogue.

The leading objective of public policy will be rapidly shifting from getting people into college to the more difficult and subtle one of making college a truly educational experience in the contemporary meaning of the term. We need a general *aggiornamento* of higher education. Beyond this, we need means of coupling the forces of innovation and experiment to the forces that influence the distribution of students among institutions.

The second, and concurrent, development will be the evolution of a much richer variety of institutions and organizational forms. The four-year college course, a legacy of the nineteenth century, even with all its recent revisions, retains a rigidity of concept, content, and method. Even its calendar is rigid. The pressure of increasing numbers has created such a massive problem that it diverts energy and attention from innovation and reform. Indeed, the temptation has been to accept the pressure for admission to college as evidence that the product is already so appealing to the customers that it stands in little need of improvement. The public habit of brand loyalty, and the mindless reliance on degrees as status symbols, have retarded the needed development of flexible forms of post-high school education. The possibilities of interfusing liberal studies with programs of vocational utility have been incompletely explored.

The large number of college students who need a change of pace and an interruption of study are poorly served by our existing procedures. Many able youngsters are "action-oriented." For them a period of purely intellectual study becomes frustrating. A year or two in a job, or in exploring several jobs, can give many of them a completely new view of life and send them back to college refreshed, with an appetite for study. Our habit of regarding a four-year course as a norm and ideal do great harm to such youngsters. They are likely to be tagged as "dropouts," or "failures," with permanent injury to the self-confidence they need and should retain. A major aspect of educational reform will have to include flexibility of timing.

All these things will come to pass, some of them sooner than we now dare hope. In the meantime the year-to-year work of recruiting, selection, and guidance will go on. To bring these processes into the central stream of education by increasing the student's awareness of the options open to him with all their values and implications will become a major preoccupation of those concerned with admissions and will inevitably involve faculties to a much greater extent than now. The concept of education in the light of the public interest must include the guidance process as an integral part of education. College teachers, it is to be hoped, will aspire to reach whatever students come before them and be less insistent that unless they can teach the most promising they would rather not teach at all. When this day comes, admissions committees, at the same time, may admit that they cannot always spot the winners, that the race is not always to the swift, and that the eager student sometimes outpaces the bright one. They may even grow more willing than now to accept with humility the duty of doing as much as they can for whatever students present themselves, in the assurance that among those who look least impressive to begin with, through the inscrutable operations of a statistical Providence, unsuspected talent will come to light.

# Notes

1. The convention of speaking of the "supply" of students coming out of the general population and the "demand" for students by colleges is adopted here arbitrarily. At the postgraduate stage, the "supply" is the annual crop emerging from the undergraduate course, and the "demand" arises from employers. The British "Robbins Report," with equal propriety, adopts the converse convention: it speaks throughout of the "demand" for education (on the part of students), and the "supply" of education (by the colleges). As in any market situation, demand and supply are opposite aspects of the same set of transactions. See Chapter 6 of *Higher Education; Report of the Committee Appointed by the Prime Minister under the Chairmanship of Lord Robbins.* London: H. M. Stationery Office, 1963, 335 PP.

2. Out of 811 admissions officers, 18 percent were found to have the title of registrar and 8 percent a title combining registrar with admissions officer in some form. Jane Zech Hauser and Paul F. Lazarsfeld, *The Admissions Officer in the American College: An Occupation under Change.* A report for the College Entrance Examination Board. New York: College Entrance Examination Board, 1963. Chapters separately paginated.

3. *Who Should Go to College.* New York: Columbia University Press, 1952, 190 pp. This was a pioneering effort. See especially the chapter by Robert J. Havighurst and Robert R. Rodgers on motivation for college attendance.

4. *After High School—What?* Minneapolis: University of Minnesota Press, 1954, 240 pp. See also R. Clyde White, *These Will Go to College.* Cleveland: Press of Western Reserve University, 1952. This is a model of workmanlike investigation of a limited area in Ohio. It was followed by many regional forecasts on similar lines.

5. See, for example, *The Search for Talent. College Admissions No. 7.* New York: College Entrance Examination Board, 1960, 131 pp.

6. Cited in note 1. This report and the discussions of it provide a useful case study of the forces at work in these situations. For a penetrating criticism of the report, see Martin Trow, "A Question of Size and Shape." *Universities Quarterly* (London), March 1964, p. 136.

7. Henry T. Hillson and Florence C. Myers, *The Demonstration Guidance Project, 1957-1962*. New York: Board of Education, 1963. This outlines the follow-up in senior high school of the original experimental groups in Junior High School No. 43.

8. Seymour E. Harris, *The Market for College Graduates and Related Aspects of Education and Income*. Cambridge, Mass.: Harvard University Press, 1949, 207 pp. Pp. 64-75 summarize these fears.

9. *The Aims of Education and Other Essays*. New York: The Macmillan Co., 1929, 247 pp. See p. 74.

10. Frank Bowles, *Access to Higher Education*. New York: Unesco and The International Association of Universities, 1963, 212 pp. This is a unique and classic study of the problem in a worldwide context.

11. See A. W. Astin, "Productivity of Undergraduate Institutions." *Science,* April 13, 1962, pp. 129-135. See also "Undergraduate Institutions and the Production of Scientists." *Science,* July 26, 1963, pp. 334-338.

12. See for example as two of the best: E. A. Wilson and C. A. Bucher, *College Ahead! A Guide for High School Students and Their Parents*. New York: Harcourt, Brace & Co., 1961, 180 pp. And Frank Bowles, *How to Get into College*. New York: E. P. Dutton & Co., Inc., 1960, 185 pp.

13. See *Admissions to Harvard College*. A Report by the Special Committee on College Admission Policy. Cambridge, Mass.: Harvard University, 1960, 56 pp.

14. George D. Spindler, "The Character Structure of Anthropology," in George D. Spindler (ed.), *Education and Culture*. New York: Holt, Rinehart and Winston, 1963, 571 pp.

15. See Alfred North Whitehead's discussion, *Adventures of Ideas*. New York: The New American Library, Inc., Mentor Books, 1955, 302 pp. Originally published by The Macmillan Company in 1933.

16. Margaret L. Habein (ed.), *Spotlight on the College Student*. Washington, D. C.: American Council on Education, 1959, 89 pp.

17. A characteristic expression of this earlier attitude appeared in G. H. Lorimer's *Letters from a Self-Made Merchant to His Son* (Boston: Small, Maynard & Co., 1903), a book that had considerable vogue at the turn of the century. For example: ". . . could prove that two and two make four by trigonometry and geometry, but couldn't learn to keep books; was as thick as thieves with all the high-toned poets, but couldn't write a good snappy merchantable streetcar ad." Philosophers of this stamp granted approval to higher education only as a strictly practical aid in business (in this case meat packing). The following passage, now

a half-century old, is a kind of "museum piece" in the light of current demands from business for educated people at a much more profound level of intellectual sophistication:

"Does a college education pay?—Does it pay to take a steer that's been running loose on the range and living on cactus and petrified wood till he's just a bunch of barbwire and sole leather, and feed him corn till he's just a solid hunk of porterhouse steak and oleo oil?

"You bet it pays. Anything that trains a boy to think and to think quick pays; anything that teaches a boy to get the answer before the other fellow gets through biting the pencil pays.

"College doesn't make fools; it develops them. It doesn't make bright men; it develops them."

18. See, for example, articles by various authors on elementary science courses in the *Quarterly Report* of Educational Services, Inc., Watertown, Massachusetts, Winter-Spring, 1964, pp. 61-82.

19. See William C. Fels, "The College Describes Itself." *College Board Review* No. 38, Spring 1959, pp. 30-32. This masterpiece of gentle satire should be read by anyone who expects to write admissions literature.

20. This elegant formulation of the nub of the student's problem is taken from Martin Katz, *Decisions and Values: A Rationale for Secondary School Guidance.* New York: College Entrance Examination Board, 1963, 67 pp. See p. 25.

21. Daniel Lerner in *The Passing of Traditional Society* documents these tensions in realistic detail. Glencoe, Ill.: The Free Press of Glencoe (now a division of The Macmillan Co., New York), 466 pp.

22. See Frank Bowles, *Access to Higher Education,* cited in note 10. This pioneering study analyzes in detailed variety the social forces that have sometimes encouraged but usually hindered the movement of able students into universities in many countries.

23. Simon Newcomb, *The Reminiscences of an Astronomer.* Boston: Houghton Mifflin Company, 1903.

24. See especially James B. Conant, *Slums and Suburbs: A Commentary on Schools in Metropolitan Areas.* New York: McGraw-Hill Book Co., Inc., 1961, 147 pp.

25. The literature on racial discrimination is immense. Especially recommended are: Robert L. Sutherland, *Color, Class, and Personality,* 1942, 135 pp.; Allison Davis and John Dollard, *Children of Bondage,* 1940, 299 pp.; and W. L. Warner, B. H. Junker, and W. A. Adams, *Color and Human Nature,* 1941, 301 pp. All three of these studies were published by the American Council on Education,

26. Nevitt Sanford's compendium, *The American College,* reflects in a number of passages recurring doubts about the effectiveness of many current educational practices. New York: John Wiley & Sons, Inc., 1962, 1,084 pp. See note 27.

27. This literature ranges from the impressionistic but useful sketches of David Boroff, through the penetrating sociological comparisons of different colleges by Everett C. Hughes (for example: "How Colleges Differ," pp. 16-22 in *Planning College Policy for the Critical Decade Ahead. College Admissions No. 5.* New York: College Entrance Examination Board, 1958, 116 pp.), to the more rigorous psychological characterizations by C. R. Pace (for example: "Five College Environments." *College Board Review* No. 41, Spring 1960, pp. 24-28). Among the classics in this general area are David Riesman's *Constraint and Variety in American Education.* (New York: Doubleday & Co., 1958, 174 pp.); and *The American College,* edited by Nevitt Sanford (see note 26).

28. Edwin Cornelius Broome, *A Historical and Critical Discussion of College Admission Requirements.* 1903. Reprinted by the College Entrance Examination Board, New York, 1963, 157 pp.

29. *Ibid.,* p. 130 ff.

30. The Association of College Admissions Counselors, now an influential national organization, had its origins in this period, when an urgent need became apparent for a "code of ethics" to regulate intense competitive recruiting efforts, particularly among midwestern colleges. The later broadening of the organization to include secondary schools, as well as its geographical diversification, gave it increased standing as a Level Three project.

31. In the 1950s a vigorous movement for better communication and closer relationships between colleges and secondary schools was initiated. One important focus of this effort was the Secondary School-College Relations Committee of the American Association of Collegiate Registrars and Admissions Officers. See for example the 1955 AACRAO booklet, *Secondary School–College Co-operation, an Obligation to Youth.*

32. A classic account of the advantages and problems of school-college teacher exchange is Edwin Fenton's "Working with High Schools: A Professor's Testimony." *The School Review,* Vol. 69, No. 2, Summer 1961, pp. 157-168.

33. See Jane Zech Hauser and Paul F. Lazarsfeld's *The Admissions Officer . . .,* cited in note 2.

34. An admirable example of determined faculty effort to wrestle with some of the insoluble dilemmas is *Admission to Harvard College,* cited in note 13. See also pp. 52-73 of the "Annual Report of the Admission and Scholarship Committee,"

in *Report of the President of Harvard College, 1959-60,* for Dean Wilbur Bender's discussion of some of these problems.

35. See particularly Henry S. Dyer, "Ambiguity in Selective Admissions." *Journal of the Association of College Admissions Counselors,* Fall 1963, p. 15 ff.

36. See Mary E. Chase, "The Admissions Counselor—Guide or Gambler?" *College Board Review* No. 27, Fall 1955, pp. 25-28.

37. See Joshua A. Fishman and Ann K. Pasanella, "College Admission-Selection Studies." *Review of Educational Research,* October 1960, Vol. XXX, No. 4, pp. 298-310. See especially the bibliography.

38. I am indebted to Henry B. Phillips for his original thought along these lines. See his paper, "On the Nature of Progress." *American Scientist,* Autumn 1945, Vol. 33, No. 4, pp. 253-259.

39. See Frank Bowles, 1963, cited in note 10. This study assembles striking evidence of the severe restriction of educational opportunity in many countries.

40. Cited in note 2.

41. See B. A. Thresher, "Using Admissions Information in College Counseling," pp. 53-63 in *Counseling in School and College. College Admissions No. 8.* New York: College Entrance Examination Board, 1961, 71 pp.

42. See especially J. Roswell Gallagher, "The Role of the Emotions in Academic Success," pp. 106-109 in *College Admissions No. 1.* New York: College Entrance Examination Board, 1954, 156 pp. And Dana L. Farnsworth, "Some Non-Academic Causes of Success and Failure in College Students," pp. 72-78 in *College Admissions No. 2.* New York: College Entrance Examination Board, 1955, 98 pp.

43. See Claude M. Fuess, *The College Board, Its First Fifty Years.* New York: Columbia University Press, 1950, 222 pp. See especially Chapters I-III.

44. See for example Byron S. Hollinshead's 1952 study, cited in note 3, and Ralph F. Berdie's *After High School—What?,* cited in note 4. These were pioneer efforts to open up the sociological aspects of access to higher education.

45. But see Louis T. Benezet, "College Admissions: The Hours before the Dawn." *A.C.A.C. Journal,* Winter 1963, Vol. 8, No. 3, p. 19. This thoughtful discussion stresses the large fraction of colleges in which the admissions officer, under pretense of selection, is in effect "selling space" in the college.

46. It is important to judge the student's motives more by what he does than what he says. The fact that about 80 percent of students attend colleges within their own state is in sharp contrast to a study that shows 52.9 percent of college males explaining their choice of a college because it was a "good college," while

18.0 percent explained their choice as "close to home." See John L. Holland, "Student Explanations of College Choice and Their Relation to College Popularity, College Productivity, and Sex Differences." *College and University,* Spring 1958, Vol. 33, No. 3, pp. 313-320. There is ample evidence that for most students few colleges other than those nearby come into consideration. See for example David Riesman, "College Subcultures and College Outcomes," pp. 1-14 in *Selection and Educational Differentiation.* Berkeley, Calif.: Center for the Study of Higher Education, 1959, 187 pp.

47. This theme, made explicit by Robert Merton, has been elaborated by David Riesman. See for example *Constraint and Variety in American Education* (cited in note 27), pp. 25-26.

48. See A. W. Astin's articles, cited in note 11.

49. "The Distribution of 'Wealth' in Higher Education." *College and University,* Vol. 37, No. 2, Winter 1962, pp. 113-125.

50. John D. Millett, *The Academic Community.* New York: McGraw-Hill Book Co., Inc., 1962, 265 pp. See p. 125.

51. Chicago: Science Research Associates, Inc., 1965, 125 pp.